T0128135

Disband the CORRUPT Federal Reserve SYSTEM and the IRS NOW!

Pete Sotos

DISBAND THE CORRUPT FEDERAL RESERVE SYSTEM AND THE IRS NOW!

iUniverse books may be ordered through booksellers or by contacting:

iUniverse
1663 Liberty Drive
Bloomington, IN 47403
www.iuniverse.com
1-800-Authors (1-800-288-4677)

ISBN: 978-1-4917-6209-7 (sc)
ISBN: 978-1-4917-6210-3 (e)

Library of Congress Control Number: 2015903546

Print information available on the last page.

iUniverse rev. date: 3/13/2015

Chapter 1

The American people must ask their representatives and senators three major questions:

1) In what year were the Federal Reserve System and the IRS created?
2) *Who* created the Federal Reserve System and the IRS?
3) Why were the Federal Reserve System and the IRS created in the same year?

Tom Daschle, a former senator, made $5 million in lobbying. And, mind you, he forgot to pay income taxes on it. So far, I have not heard of any IRS action against this income tax evader.

Abe Lincoln said, "I fear that this form of government together with the corporations shall collude against the American people."

Source: The standard authority on Abe Lincoln's speeches and writings and the collected works of Abraham Lincoln's large multi-volume publications.

Corporations go to Washington and lobby Congress to issue legislation to favor them and not the public. Mr.

Ross Perot stated, "They can lobby, just as long as not one nickel changes hands." source: stated on tv when running for the presidency of the US.

The American people are more concerned about sports—their teams, players, and records—than with politics. They are not watching Congress. Don't they realize they will pay a dear price if they don't? They are now paying that price. We are enslaved through illegal and excessive taxation. Legislators steal income tax money in various ways. Most are lawyers and can con us simply because the people are uneducated and ignorant.

The newly elected officials—Walker, Rubio, Ryan, Cruz, Paul, West, and so on—appear to be on the right track. These people were elected because of the efforts of the Tea Party. This book is all about *causation*. How did it all come about? How did these happenings occur in our history?

Franklin D. Roosevelt said, "Nothing happens by accident. It is all well planned and then executed."

Is it a little suspicious that two world wars happened after 1913? Are the Rothschilds at work in the United States?

It is important for the Tea Party to address our humongous debt problem. However, it is even more important to vigorously attack the illegality of the feds and the IRS. Congress continues to play games by lowering or raising taxes and debt. They will not stop the spending because Congress plays politics all the time. They fight each other like children, and absolutely nothing gets done. For this reason—and many other reasons—we must take the helm or perish financially.

Americans must lead the way by stopping excess spending. They have caused their own misery by spending more than they earn—just as the government does. They can't figure out that debt is financial cancer that will destroy them. One *must* live within one's means. Save, pay in cash, and haggle over prices. Many people buy used items that work very well for them.

I have no credit cards. I live well within my means and invest the difference to increase my *unearned* income. What about you?

The Tea Party voted out a lot of the incumbents in 2008 and took control of the House and the Senate. This is a major step in forcing Congress to stop spending and debt limit increases. This process must be repeated. Disband the Federal Reserve System and IRS, and replace the IRS with a national retail sales tax system. Why? When I buy a car, I know what I got for my sales tax (a car). When I buy clothing, I know what I got for my sales tax (clothing). This will be very difficult for us to execute because it will take away the control of our money by Congress through *taxation*.

I would set the sales tax at 15 percent for all items except food and 20 percent for luxury items. Luxury items include jewelry, furs, expensive cars, yachts, airplanes, multimillion-dollar homes, artifacts, and paintings.

Moreover, we will keep 100 percent of what we earn, sell, and win. We will know exactly how much we will be paying in taxes based upon our purchases. Most workers who earn minimum wage will obtain items from garage sales, swap meets, and thrift stores without paying any sales tax. The sales tax on very old vehicles will be insignificant, and people must save to pay for them.

Furthermore, we will have a huge nationwide pool of disposable income. We can pay off debt and invest money in the stock market and real estate—once we study those difficult, risky investments. People have to learn how to handle the profits from investments. I call this *unearned income*. Never spend your investment principal—only spend the income it creates. The more people invest, the more unearned income they will enjoy.

Most people will not do this. Most people will continue to spend it all. Spending is a no-brainer. This will be good for the subgovernments, because sales taxes will soar. The increase in revenue will help states expand services to the population.

Chapter 2

Answering the Three Questions

Who created the Federal Reserve System and IRS legislation? Evil bankers met secretly on Jekyll Island, which is off the coast of Georgia, in November 1910. The top-secret meeting was allegedly for a nine-day duck hunt. These evil bankers included J. P. Morgan, Paul Warburg, Jacob Schiff, Frank A. Vanderlip (protégé of John D. Rockefeller), and Bernard Baruch. Senator Nelson Aldrich came from Newport, Rhode Island, to represent the wealthiest bankers in the country. They rode in Aldrich's private rail car to the Georgia transfer point to Jekyll Island.

Why were the Federal Reserve System and the IRS created at the same time? In 1913, in order to pay for highly profitable and costly wars, the people had to be taxed at any limit. They were *forced* to pay the tax. In addition, the banking system had to be controlled by a private system in order to control the nation's money and economy. The system would have no checks or balances. The government still controls our entire banking system and the economy.

Chapter 3

The Devastating Effects of Taxation

The evil bankers conned Congress into giving the power to the IRS to incarcerate anyone who did not pay income taxes. With this power in place, Congress could vote to substantially increase income taxes.

Think I'm kidding? Think again. What were the highest tax rates in the late fifties and early sixties? Can you believe they were 94 percent, 92 percent, and 88 percent? That was the major reason why Ronald Reagan ran for the presidency in 1980. He lowered the federal income tax rate from 70 percent to 50 percent.

Prior to 1986 tax act, 60 percent of capital gains were exempt from being taxed. The career criminals killed this loophole in 1986 and taxed 100 percent of capital gains. Many other loopholes were closed, substantially raising our *overall* tax burden in the Tax Reform Act of 1986. When those thug legislators used the word *loophole*, it was a tax advantage for the American people. When Congress eliminates a loophole, they in effect increase our taxes. This is why these congressional thugs must be voted out of office forever.

The American people must understand that new legislation created by Congress each year is to close the loopholes, thereby increasing our tax burden. This is an illegal method to literally steal our money. All expenditures and taxation is over a ten-year period. They never conform to this period of time. Every year, there is a new Congress—and all is forgotten or paid lip service too. Most people don't do their income tax returns, and they are oblivious about taxation and the congressional acts each year the new Congress convenes.

It is noted that about 40 to 50 percent of the taxpayers do not pay any income taxes. So why should they study or care about income taxes. Those who do pay income taxes could avoid much taxation if they talked to a CPA and learn how to minimize their tax burdens.

Congress declared income tax for individuals *unconstitutional* in 1895 and *unconstitutional* for corporations in 1909. So what happened? What did US Supreme Court Justice John Marshall Harlan have to say after the Pre-Pollock and Pollock cases? In part, if both the courts and governments are so opposed to the definition of income taxes, then there is *no basis of law* to adjudge anyone on this subject of income taxation.

The IRS lost the Amy T. Critzer case. She was an eastern Cherokee who was accused by the IRS of criminally evading income taxes from 1967 to 1970. The case went all the way to the Supreme Court, and Justice John Marshall Harlan completely exonerated her of all charges.

The IRS never talks about the cases they lose. In my professional opinion, Harlan's legal opinion still stands today. The IRS was also caught in a criminal situation by falsifying documents and accusing businessmen of underpaying income taxes. There were so many complaints by these businessmen to Congress that Congress set up a committee to investigate it. Senator Bill Ross of Maryland chaired the committee. He was appropriately elected to chair the committee with his LLM and MBA degrees in taxation.

In the 1990s, the committee interviewed six IRS agents. Three were retired, and three were still employed by the IRS. The IRS agents had an average of thirty-five years of experience. All had their backs to the TV to avoid being identified by the IRS. If the IRS were honest, why would they fire employees for telling the truth?

All six agents admitted to falsification. Jerome Kurt, the IRS commissioner, and others were fired. Charles Rossetti was appointed acting IRS commissioner. The IRS is illegal, and it functions illegally. Moreover, it could not account for two-thirds of the money it took in after an audit from the Government Accounting Office (GAO). All of our checks are now made payable to the US Treasury and not the IRS. Check your tax return to see who the payee was.

By voting these career criminal legislators into office time and again, the American people have subjected themselves to poverty. Most have only enough money to buy the bare necessities and have nothing left over to save or invest.

If the IRS were disbanded, there would be no income tax returns. This means that nothing would be taxed or deducted. The costs to taxpayers in keeping records and fighting the IRS in court are enormous. What one earns, one keeps. Now we have awesome disposable income. We can pay off all of our debts and have plenty left over to invest. We complete the national retail sales tax by adding the states that don't have it. This will be a state function, and they will take care of it.

With the sales tax at 15 percent and 20 percent for luxury items, many Americans would continue to spend, which would bode well for all of us, because sales taxes would soar. This would give our subgovernments more money to increase services as the state populations increase. This will cut the federal government down to its smallest size—as it should be. Many government functions should be state functions and not federal functions. Not one sales tax dime should go overseas. All sales tax should be for the states to use.

No more wars; killing and mutilating our youth is criminal. If we save more than $1 trillion per year, the national debt would be cut by two-thirds in ten years. A lot of our military will go to our southern border to wipe out the drug cartel. We would be doing something constructive with our military—for our country instead of for other countries.

Chapter 4

Reaganomics

In 1980 after his election, president Reagan lowered the federal income tax rate from 70 percent to 50 percent. This lowered the capital gains tax from 28 percent to 20 percent. At the time, 60 percent of capital gains were exempt from taxation. For example, if you made a $1,000 profit on a sale, only 40 percent or $400 was taxable (70 percent of $400 is $280, and 50 percent of $400 is $200), saving $80 on taxes. This is peanuts for rich people.

Let's take a painting bought for $200,000 and sold for $1 million. The tax is on the $800,000 gain, of which 60 percent is exempt from taxation, leaving a balance of $320,000 to be taxed: 70 percent of $320,000 is $224,000. The same balance of $320,000 taxed at 50 percent is $160,000, which is a savings of $64,000 in taxes. The rich can now donate to charities, universities, etc. For higher-value items that appreciate, the tax savings would be enormous.

The IRS illegally taxes many items where they had no hand in creating the gain. The same goes for prizes in game shows, lotteries, casinos, etc. We must reconstruct

Congress by voting almost all of them out of office—and then change all the rules.

Some Americans are waking up and joining the Tea Party to fight the career criminals in Congress. The Tea Party voted a lot of the incumbents out. The Tea Party elected their people and took control of the House. Next is the Senate. We can see how effective this is. The Republican Party is holding the evil Democrats at bay with taxing, spending, and debt ceiling increases.

Through the Tea Party, we must continue to replace the incumbents. It will take a strong organization to destroy them. Do yourself a favor and join the Tea Party. We must eliminate taxation; it is a license for these career criminals to steal our money.

After Reagan's tax decrease in 1980, huge interest rate increases by Fed Chairman Paul Volcker—and large tax increases by career criminal Democrats—delayed Reaganomics. Bob Dole—a Republican—went along with all of the Democratic tax increases in the eighties. This is a major problem in the Senate and the House. There is always a leader from the opposite party in concert with the other side to keep the game going of stealing from us through income taxation.

Who writes these bills and submits them to Congress? Try the IRS, legislators, and the Treasury—and please don't forget the corporations. The IRS cannot submit any bills if they are *disbanded*. The corporations can lobby, but no money changes hands as Ross Perot stated when he was a candidate for the presidency in the mid 1990's. If money changes hands, it will be a criminal offense with a huge fine and a long term of imprisonment. The legislators will not be permitted to *add on bill(s)* at the end. This is a favorite dirty trick of theirs in creating pork bucks and pocketing a lot of it. this is one of the many ways they become rich.

The sole function of the Tea Party is to get these career criminals out of office. Once, we believed that holding public office was an honor and a privilege. It was held in the highest regard because they were trustworthy. That policy is long gone. We must institute this policy again.

Chapter 5

The Federal Reserve Board and the Central Bank

Let's expose the most corrupt scheme ever devised by evil men: the Federal Reserve Board. The name itself is a deception. There is no reserve.

Are there any American banks left? There were more than 20,000 banks in the United States at the start of the 1900s. There are now less than 7,500. Currently, almost 900 are going to be closed. This means there is less money for the FDIC to collect from the banks to insure your deposits. There is more bad news. As of December 31, 2009, the FDIC was in the red. By 2014, it is estimated that the FDIC will be $52 billion in the red. The FDIC must be eliminated. It serves no purpose at this time other than fooling people that their deposits are insured up to a certain amount.

Many of us don't need a physical banking office. We can now do everything online, use ATM outlets, and find cash machines in many places.

Every time the feds close a bank, people are laid off. This means more unemployment and more foreclosures. This should be a banking activity. However, the feds control our banking system. The feds have about 22,000 employees. Disband them and get rid of a monstrous scheme that should not be. Who pays these employees? What! our government! Can't be the feds are allegedly a separate private corporation from the government. Oh, oh something is very wrong here.

On any Friday night, after all customers have left the bank, the feds come in and announce to all employees that this bank is shut down (in some cases permanently) and will reopen Monday. When the bank reopens on Monday, the Fed's employees reassure the depositors that all deposits are fully insured up to a certain limit. For the banks that cannot be merged and therefore fail, the feds announce that all employees must leave and seek new jobs. The feds were created to control our banking system, which should not be since the feds were created illegally. This should only be a banking function.

This legislation was called the Federal Reserve Act of 1913. The banker's conned Congress into thinking that a privately owned central banking system was needed to stabilize the economy and prevent inflation and economic depressions. It has time and again proven to us that this was a boldfaced lie. It has intentionally—yes, intentionally—caused inflation, economic depressions, and wars (in that order). The bankers who conned Congress have succeeded in doing so by this very act. In addition, the other powers given to the feds were:

1. raising interest rates at any time and without any limit

2. increasing or decreasing the banks' reserve limits by any percentage
3. taking money out of the banking system or put it back in electronically

There is no money involved. This is a figure created electronically by the feds to control the flow of money in our banking system.

The Federal Reserve Board has thirteen members. There are twelve Federal Reserve Banks in the country. Each bank has a president, and each president is a member of the Federal Reserve Board. With the chairman, there are thirteen members. Seven of these members, in rotation, are appointed as board of governors, and two are appointed for a fourteen-year period by the president.

The president of the United States appoints the chairman of the Federal Reserve Board for a period of four years and can reappoint him or her for two additional four-year periods. The chairman must have an economic degree. The feds meet secretly, and I would love to be at those secret meetings. They meet about six times per year. Do the feds want to control our banks and economy that much?

There is nothing secret in the US about our businesses. The stockholders of a closely held company cannot be secret. Most businesses in the US are closely held, meaning that all workers know each other in the business. All owners or stockholders are known to the department of corporations and must file a certificate annually to note any changes in ownership, board members, or stockholders.

In the annual filing of the certificate, one must be named as "process of service." Since a firm can't be sued, a lawsuit must be given to a human who can respond to it. That's the dude named in the "process of service" question.

In a publicly held company, the stockholders do not know each other. There are thousands of them located perhaps all over the world. Moreover, many sell or buy stock on a daily basis and their identities are not important. Naturally, the officers, board members, and major stockholders are known and can easily be identified.

Evil bankers and others gave the Federal Reserve Board three awesome powers: raise or lower interest rates, raise or lower bank reserves, and electronically put in or take out money from our banking system by buying or selling Treasury bonds.

When one of the twelve Federal Reserve Banks is under its legal reserve limit, it *must* borrow money from one of the other eleven Federal Reserve Banks. At what rate of interest? The thirteen-member group determines this. This is called the federal funds rate. The federal funds rate is watched very closely by the stockbrokerage firms, giving them a direction as to where interest rates are headed—up or down.

The twelve Federal Reserve Banks loan money electronically to the money center banks. The money center banks are Bank of America, Mellon, Citigroup,

JPMorgan Chase, Wells Fargo, etc. The federal discount rate is the lowest rate given to the best borrowers, such as the large publicly held firms and other large firms.

If the interest rates go up, money becomes tight—and more costly to obtain. Corporations stop expanding and stop hiring. Keen competition prevents them from raising prices. They now resort to layoffs. The two biggest outlays for a firm are salaries and benefits. This lower outlay is more in line with reduced revenue. Our subgovernment and government do not do this unless forced to, which is currently the case. The officials wait till it is too late. Look at the bankrupt cities, counties, and states—not to mention the federal government.

The second power of the Federal Reserve Board is the scheme to lower or raise the banks' reserve limits. If the feds raise the reserve limit by only 1 percent, banks will be under their legal reserve limit. They will be shut down if this is not corrected.

The banks must scramble for bucks. They must sell some of the securities in their portfolios, call in revolving business loans, stop increases to credit card holders and loans to borrowers, and make it more costly for the few who can borrow. This is the deadly *fractional reserve system*. Our banking system in reality has very little money on hand because of this ten-to-one deposit method.

Our banks are controlled by the feds. If loans are by and large eliminated, then our banking system becomes very illiquid and can collapse. Currently, banks are stuck with huge mortgage loans that are not being paid. They can only sell the foreclosed homes to those who have the money and are in very strong financial positions to do so. There are millions of foreclosed homes and homes valued under the mortgage amounts. This will take many years to overcome. The only way that is possible is to give the American people much higher incomes in order to qualify under the strict banking rules that now exist. Income is one thing—where are the assets?

Many banks can't scramble enough to reach their increased limits, and they are shut down. Having more banks shut down, causes more layoffs and foreclosures, exacerbated this problem. At the same time, it decreased tax revenues for our subgovernments and the federal government, which caused more layoffs. This created more tax and fee increases, which caused high inflation. One can now see the destructive power this corrupt Federal Reserve Board has caused by our bribed bankers and international bankers who bribed them in the first place.

The third scheme of the Federal Reserve Board is the ability to affect the amount of money in our banking system. They can totally destroy the economy by withdrawing money from the banking system in unlimited amounts or cause inflation by putting large amounts of money into our banking system. We are now in a period called *stagflation.* This is a period of continued inflation, declining business activity, and increasing unemployment.

America's growth rate is about 2 percent. The growth rate in China is about 7 percent. Shouldn't we be at 7 percent? Is something wrong? Are the feds strangling us economically?

We are in a very deep depression. In my sixty years in the stock market, I have never seen city, county, state, and federal governments as bankrupt as they are now. I have advised my clients to keep cold cash handy. Money belts or pouches are not bad ideas.

The US has had double-digit inflation only three times in history: in 1974, with the alleged gas crisis, and in 1980 and 1981, with the alleged oil crises.

In a short period at that time, Paul Volcker, the Fed chairman, raised interest rates to 21.5 percent. He knew the banks were collecting interest on mortgages rates as low as 2, 3, and 4 percent in the seventies. How could banks possibly pay dividends that were equal to such a high interest rate? They couldn't, and Volcker knew it. He put thousands of banks out of business. He also destroyed the two largest industries at the same time. The real estate and automobile industries went broke, and tens of thousands of people left those two industries without jobs. These two industries employed the bulk of people in this country. The monster, Volcker, cured double-digit inflation, but in doing so, he killed jobs for thousands of people.

Chapter 6

The Stock Market and the Federal Reserve Board

From 1966 until 1982, we were in a sixteen-year bear market. A bear market results when all stocks go down in price. All stocks are killed, and none survive. All the homes that Levitt and Sons built in Long Island, New York, were put up for sale.

Volcker had to stop the destruction he caused. The rich, evil bankers could buy the assets for pennies on the dollar. On August 13, 1982, Volcker lowered the interest rate by 450 basis points in *one day*. Even at 17 percent, no one could qualify to buy a car or a home.

In that bear market, the Dow Jones Industrial Average period was locked in at about a thousand points at best. Every time it reached that level, it collapsed. Every time the S&P 500 reached 100 points, it collapsed.

Volcker's huge drop in interest rates caused the Dow to soar 200 points to 1200, and it didn't stop climbing until the end of the decade. Interest rates continued to decline, and the stock market continued to climb. The only pause was the crash on October 19, 1987, which was caused by the constant Democratic tax increases in the eighties, including the Tax Reform Act of 1986.

The subterfuge in the Tax Reform Act of 1986 was the two tax brackets they gave us instead of the six that had existed previously. The liars in Congress called this a tax decrease. Most of the loopholes were repealed, substantially increasing people's overall tax burden. We cannot have these liars in Congress. We must vote them out. I personally read the entire 3,700-page Tax Reform Act of 1986 and did hotel seminars about it after it was enacted. Each week, I would update my CCH tax manuals, and I could easily keep up with the current tax codes and proposed changes of tax laws.

This is how the corrupt Federal Reserve Board controls our banking system. They must be eradicated. The mere mention of interest rates being raised will send the stock market into a tailspin (and bond portfolios as well). In December of 1994, Alan Greenspan, the Fed chairman, stated that he would raise interest rates the next year, and the Dow lost ninety-six points. Greenspan consistently raised the interest rates in a lockstep fashion, and he destroyed the economy and the stock market. Do we need these monsters?

We cannot have such awesome power in so few hands. Congress knows what is going on and can act in advance for personal gain as they do.

Remember the distinction I made between the Federal Reserve Board and its secret meetings? Could it be that the secret, privately owned central bankers met with the Federal Reserve Board to tell them what to do? If we disband the feds, there will be no secret meetings.

Paying off our current government debt is *impossible* without reforming our banking system. Congress wants the American people to think the Federal Reserve Board operates in our best interests. The truth is that the Federal Reserve Board is privately owned and run purely for profit.

Chapter 7

What Important Men Had to Say about the Federal Reserve System

Why doesn't Congress act upon the Federal Reserve System and check on its legality? Most people do not understand the system. Most congressmen and senators are lawyers and do not have degrees in finance or economics. The few who did know about it were bribed and refused to talk, including Senator Nelson Aldrich.

However, a few congressmen did talk. In 1923, Rep. Charles A. Lindbergh (father of the famous aviator Lucky Lindy) said, "The financial system has been turned over to the Federal Reserve Board. That board administers the finance system by a purely profiteering group. The system is private, and they meet in secrecy. It is conducted for the sole purpose of obtaining the greatest possible profits from the use of other people's money."

Wake up! What is happening today? You can't get a loan, refinance your loans, or get a credit card. You pay the highest interest rate possible, as well as late charges, fees, and missing payments, which will destroy your credit rating. Why should anybody have credit cards? Before credit cards came about, we had to save to buy an icebox or make any other large purchase.

Chapter 8

The FICO System Is an Outright Fraud

The three credit rating agencies—Experian, Transunion, and Equifax—were named in class action lawsuits, and all three lost. I was involved in the first one. The lawsuits were because of so many public complaints about straightening out the horrific lies and mistakes the three agencies made and refused to correct—no matter how hard the public tried.

The banks use dozens of excuses and outright lies to discredit you. They know that giving you a lower FICO score will increase your loan's interest rate. This is done unlawfully to extract more money from millions of borrowers. You are undoubtedly aware of these three agencies. The banks use the following lies or excuses: too many credit cards (a lie), are they being paid on time, yes. Limits are too high, (a lie), are they being paid on time, yes. Too many inquires (nonsense) has nothing to do with payment record. Have no credit cards, (a lie), can't check your payment record. Paid off your credit cards (a lie), can't check our payment records because waited too long to reapply.

These statements by the banks are a form of blackmail. Moreover, the bank can increase interest rates at will. No wonder our forefathers hated banks and did not want them at all. As it now stands, the three credit agencies are charged with fraud again and are now being investigated.

There is an old adage: once a crook, always a crook. Equifax, the worst of the three, was sued successfully to the tune of $18.6 million for unlawfully destroying a woman's credit and identity completely.

New legislation was adopted in favor of the corporations, just as Lincoln stated. One such recent regulation was Regulation D of the banking act about 2009. If you had more than six transactions in your saving accounts, you would be charged fees for each additional transaction. This is stealing your money! Wake up and vote the politicians who supported this bill out of office. One can learn which legislators voted for which bill. This is a matter of record. People can also watch the actual voting process live on C-SPAN 1 or 2.

Remember, banks create money out of thin air. They use the fractional reserve method and have the audacity to have you pay principal and interest back. No one should borrow money; people must live within their means. That is what savings accounts are for.

We are paying these career criminals to allow corporations to *steal* our money. The corporations pay hundreds of millions of dollars in bribes to Congress—*lobbying*—for this legislation and other legislation that is in favor of them and not us.

Chapter 9

Other Important Men in History

President James Madison said, "History records that the money changers have used every form of abuse, intrigue, deceit, and violent means possible to maintain their control over governments by controlling money and its issuance."

By World War I, the money changers had seized control of most of Europe's banks. This was smokescreened by the feds in the media. How do we fix this? We must issue and control our own money.

Thomas Jefferson, Andrew Jackson, Abe Lincoln, and Martin Van Buren understood the awesome powers that were given to the privately owned central banks. It is now the most powerful privately owned central banking system in the world.

As a matter of fact, it controls all—yes, all—of the money in the world through its privately owned central banks.

Two thousand years ago in Jerusalem, one particular coin—the half shekel—was the only acceptable coin in the Jewish community. However, the money changers raised the price of the coin and made enormous profits since they had a virtual monopoly on the gold coins. The Jewish community had no choice but to pay that price or have little or no money for goods and necessities.

Chapter 10

The Goldsmiths

The money changers (now called goldsmiths) bought and took other people's gold under the cunning guise of safekeeping. The people were given paper certificates for their gold and silver. This caught on because it was more convenient to carry paper than heavy gold or silver coins.

The goldsmiths noticed that only a small fraction of the depositors wanted their gold at any one time. This meant that the goldsmiths could print more money from the gold they had on deposit. Using other people's gold, no one would be the wiser.

In the Middle Ages, lending money and collecting interest was called usury. It reduced the value of every one's money.

The goldsmiths would loan out the money and collect interest on it. This method was called *fractional reserve lending.* In other words, they could loan out more money than they had on deposit by using other people's gold as a reserve. For each $1,000 on deposit, they could lend out about $10,000 and collect interest on it. No one would discover the process.

The goldsmiths used this wealth to accumulate more and more gold. Today, the banks can loan out ten times more money than they have on hand. They charge 8 percent interest—actually, it's 80 percent interest. The banks made 8 percent interest on the money they had on hand. The banks create more money by using the *fractional reserve lending scheme* and lending that out at 8 percent interest. Ten times 8 percent equals 80 percent. Paying high interest rates is a burden on businesses.

The goldsmiths have learned how to make money between *easy* money and *tight* money. They would increase the money supply, inflation, or *easy* money as it became plentiful. People took out loans to expand their businesses, and individuals bought homes, furnishings, cars, etc. Now they are deep in debt.

The money changers then *tightened* the money supply to make loans more difficult to get. Less money in circulation means the banks will become very picky about to who can obtain a loan. The masses are now in a bind. They could not refinance loans or obtain more credit and went bankrupt. They sold their assets for pennies on the dollar just to survive.

The same thing is going on right now!

Economists refer to this up-down movement of the economy as the business cycle. Few economists knew what was really going on with the feds and the IRS manipulating our economy. These economists used various economic models to try to figure out where the economy is headed. This is a very difficult subject to undertake in college, and very few do because it is all theory and very difficult to understand.

CHAPTER 11

THE TALLY STICK SYSTEM

In AD 1100, King Henry VIII resolved to take the money away from the goldsmiths by using just about anything for money, including seashells, just as they did in ancient Tibet.

The king created the tally stick system. He used a scalloped wooden stick about six feet long to represent 25,000 pounds of gold. This measuring stick could be used to manipulate the goldsmiths. The king used the stick to purchase gold from the most powerful bank in the world, the Bank of England.

The tally stick system succeeded, despite constant attacks by the money changers. The money changers offered coins as competition. In other words, coins never went out of circulation. The coins were good for the payment of taxes. Finally, King Henry VIII relaxed the laws concerning usury in the 1500s. The money changers wasted no time in asserting themselves. They made gold and silver plentiful for a few decades.

Queen Mary took the throne and tightened the usury laws, and the nation plunged into an economic depression. The usury law is the banking practice of lending money and charging interest on it. Queen Mary made it more difficult for the banks to loan money. Having less money in circulation deprived the people and started an economic depression.

The money changers were immediately allowed to consolidate their financial plans. For approximately the next fifty years, the money changers put their plans into action by plunging England into a series of costly and continuous wars with France. The money changers purchased a square mile in the financial center of London for their headquarters. It is still known as one of the financial centers of the world.

Chapter 12

The Bank of England

By the end of the 1600s, England was in financial ruin. Fifty years or more at war with France had done it. The Central Reserve Bank of England created money out of nothing. This was the world's first privately owned central bank. The deception was to call it the Bank of England, when it had nothing to do with the country. Like any other bank, it sold shares to get started. Unknown investors would put up 1.25 million pounds in gold to buy shares in the bank, but only 750,000 pounds were ever received by the unknown investors. Despite that, the bank started loaning money several more times than it had—all at interest. This was illegal because the bank would have to receive the 1.25 million pounds or re-charter its document.

Our government sells bonds to raise capital because they don't have the political will to raise taxes. The amount of these bonds increases, which increases our debt limit. Where is our government going to get the money to pay the interest—let alone the principal? The interest currently cost us eighteen cents on every dollar our government takes in. This is why our government is $18 trillion in debt. More money in circulation causes inflation and makes your money worth less.

The beauty of the plan is that maybe one person in a thousand can figure it out because it is hidden behind complex economic *gibberish*. Have you ever listened to Greenspan talk? Whew! When the congressional committee asks a few dumb questions, they get more gibberish from Greenspan as an answer. The session ends, and Congress is as clueless about the economy as they were before the meeting started.

CHAPTER 13

THE FORMATION OF THE BANK OR ENGLAND

With the formation of the Bank of England, the nation was soon awash in money. Massive loans were granted for almost any scheme the government could imagine. By 1698, government debt grew from 1.25 million pounds to 16 million pounds.

Naturally, taxes were increased—and increased again—to pay for all this. A series of booms and busts followed—the very thing the central banks claimed to prevent. This is exactly what has happened today, on a much grander scale, in the United States. The few who have lived within their means and put money aside will be able to buy assets for pennies on the dollar. These are the next millionaires. It is not what you earn—but what you *get to keep*.

Eddie George, the governor of the Bank of England, stated that this was needed for the stability of the nation. The bank reopened its doors in 1783 under the full control of the Rothschilds. Prior to that point, the Bank of England merely loaned money and received interest on it. The previous stockholders had no ambitious gains, but the Rothschilds did.

CHAPTER 14

THE RISE OF THE ROTHSCHILDS

It was stated in financial circles that the Rothschilds were the wealthiest family in the world. In fact, it was said they owned half of the world's wealth in the 1700 and 1800s.

Mayer Amschel Bauer decided to change his name to Rothschild. He was born in 1744 in Frankfurt, Germany, and died in 1812. Rothschild knew that lending money to kings and governments was far more profitable than lending money to wealthy individuals or corporations. Government loans are larger, and the nation's taxes back them. This is the *only reason why taxation was created* thousands of years ago. Today, in America, taxation is used to steal our money from us. Where is Congress's budget? This is why there is no budget. What is the government doing with our tax money? I can't tell because there is no budget. The Muslim puppet in the WH gave the previous dictator of Egypt 4 of our newest jets EACH costing $32 million dollars. Did we get a check for this sale that we paid for. Hell no. Wheres the beef?

Mayer Amschel Bauer served a three-year apprenticeship in Hanover, Germany at the Bank of

Oppenheim. Mayer Amschel became involved with Baron Von Estorff (the principal advisor to Landgrave Frederick II of Hesse). Landgrave was the wealthiest man in Europe. Baron advised Landgrave that Mayer Amschel had an uncanny ability to increase money through his investments. Landgrave immediately sent for him.

At the time, King George III was trying to put down the American rebellion. Mayer Amschel had King George III hire 16,800 Hessian soldiers from Landgrave. The sudden death of Landgrave at age twenty-five in 1785 gave Mayer Amschel absolute influence over his successor, Elector Wilhelm I. Both were born in 1744. Landgraves death put Mayer Amschel in charge of the largest fortune in Europe.

Mayer Amschel placed a large red shield over the door of the house he shared with the Schiff family. He took the name Rothschild from the sign. This was a five-story house in the financial center of England. The Rothschilds became the ruling power of Europe. They rose to such political power as to become the dictators of Europe. This became a secret to the public world.

Mayer Amschel sent his five sons to major cities in Europe to open branches in the family's banking business. His ultimate plan was to take over the Bank of England and use it as the lead bank. It became the first privately owned central bank.

Upon Mayer Rothschild's death in 1812, he left one billion francs to his five sons. The eldest, Anselm, was placed in charge of the Frankfurt Bank in Germany.

Anselm had no children, and the bank was later closed. The second son, Salomon, was sent to Vienna. He took over the banking monopoly that had been shared by five Jewish families. The third son, Nathan, was sent to London. Karl, the fourth son, went to Naples, and he became involved in the Alta Vendita group. The youngest son, James, founded the French branch in Paris. The five sons began their operations in government finance.

The plan was to create loan demands by taking part in the creation of financial panics, economic depressions, famines, wars, and revolutions. They succeeded very well in doing so. They made money in the great crashes—and the great wars that followed—while others lost their money and assets.

To perpetuate their wealth, they could not marry outside of the family. They had to intermarry and form no marital unions outside the family. A council of the heads of the houses met in Frankfurt in 1826, and they all approved the rule.

The Bank of England was used as a model for the same type of banks in Europe. At age twenty-one in 1798. Nathan—the smartest of them all—was sent to London. Nathan loaned England 60 million in 1819. From 1818–1832, Nathan issued eight other loans totaling $105,400,000, and subsequently issued eighteen other loans totaling 700 million.

The Rothschilds soon dominated Europe's banking industry. This remained a secret to the public world as they hired trusted agents to do their bidding. They also controlled the gold and diamond mines of South

Africa, knowing that gold was scarce and could easily be controlled.

By 1850, James Rothschild, the heir to the family fortunes, was said to be worth 600 million francs. This was about 250 million more francs than all the bankers in France. The Rothschilds created a very long war against the Russian imperial family. The Russian family's name was derived from Roma Nova, meaning new Rome. Prince Prus, brother of Emperor August of Rome, founded Russia in 1614. Michael became the first Romanov czar. After the fall of Napoleon, the Rothschilds turned against the Romanovs. In 1825, the Rothschilds poisoned and assassinated the rulers. The Red Guards looted the Imperial Bank building in Moscow.

The Red Guards took the imperial jewel collection and 700 million in gold. The loot was worth more than $1 billion. They also confiscated land from the czar. Moreover, there were enormous cash reserves that the czar had in European and American banks. Between 1905 and 1910, the czar sent more than 900 million to be deposited in leading New York banks, such as Chase, National City, J. P. Morgan, Hanover, and Manufacturers Trust. The Rothschilds controlled these banks through their American agents, J. P. Morgan and Kuhn, Loeb Company, which was created by Jacob Schiff after he married an American women Nina Loeb.

These banks bought control of the Federal Reserve Bank of New York in 1914 and have held the stock ever since. In addition, huge sums in English banks were never disbursed by those banks. This gave the Rothschilds the chance to take control of huge sums of money. The compounding principal and interest amounted to more than $50 billion.

In 1785, Mayer Amschel Rothschild moved his family into a very large five-story home. The Schiff family was close by. The two families intermarried, and soon both families were playing a major role in the banking business in Europe and America.

In America, the Rothschilds financed J. P. Morgan, Rockefeller, Vanderbilt, Carnegie, and other wealthy individuals. At the time of World War I, J. P. Morgan was thought to be the wealthiest man in America. However, after his death, in Rome on March 31, 1913, it was discovered that he was only a tenant of the Rothschild family. It was also discovered that he owned only 19 percent of the J. P. Morgan Company.

Chapter 15

The American Revolution

In America, the colonies had an extreme shortage of gold coins. England had passed a law that required people to pay taxes with gold or silver coins. The idea now was for the colonies to create money. The colonies began to issue their own money, which was not backed by gold or silver. It was a totally fiat (new) currency.

In 1764, England passed the Currency Act. The colonies could only use gold or silver coins to pay the taxes to England. Ben Franklin stated, "In one year, the conditions were so reversed that the era of prosperity ended and a depression set in to such an extent that the streets of the colonies were filled with the unemployed." This was the basic cause of the revolution.

In Benjamin Franklin's autobiography, he explained that the economy would have borne the little tax on tea and other matters, if not for the fact that England, made the colonies script money worthless, which created unemployment and dissatisfaction. The colonies were unable to get the power to issue their own money permanently out of the hands of George III and the international bankers.

By the time the first shot was fired at Fort Sumter in Lexington, Massachusetts, on April 19, 1775, the colonies were drained of gold and silver coins.

The colonies had no choice but to print their own money to finance the war. At the start of the American Revolution, the money supply was only $12 million. By the end of the war, the twelve million would soar to $500 million. Obviously, the colonies did not realize the deadly effects of too much money, which would cause extreme inflation. The currency became virtually worthless. It cost $5,000 to buy a pair of shoes. Inflation was so bad that George Washington said you would need a wagon load of money just to buy a wagon load of provisions.

The colonial script worked so well only two decades earlier that the Bank of England outlawed it.

Chapter 16

The Bank of North America

In 1781, dollars were needed at the end of the war. Boy, did the Constitution bungle this problem. The colonial leaders allowed Robert Morse to open a privately owned central bank in America. Morse became wealthy by selling war material as our leaders are now doing under the false pretense that we are the leaders of the free world. We are in fact the rulers of the free world because we sell the war materials to these countries and our politicians pocket the money.

The Bank of North America was closely modeled after the Bank of England. It was allowed to practice fractional reserve lending. The bank would lend out money it created—over and above the deposits on hand—and would charge interest on it. They had the audacity to make the borrower pay the interest and principal on the loan. If you or I did that, we would be charged with fraud a felony.

The bank's charter required it to have $400,000 of initial capital. Morse was unable to raise it. Morse used the gold deposited in the bank as a reserve to borrow the needed capital. Morse brazenly used his influence to use the gold deposited in the bank to create loans.

Morse then loaned himself and his friends the money to reinvest in the bank and buy their shares of stock to create the bank.

As with the Bank of England, the Bank of North America had a monopoly of the nation's currency. This type of central bank is very different from our banks that service our financial needs. It is designed to control all of our banks and the monetary system. That is why it has to be privately owned by secret stockholders that are outside the reach of the government's checks and balances. The value of American currency continued to plummet. Four years later, in 1785, the Bank of North America's charter was not renewed.

Only six years later, three men organized to form a new bank, using their influence to ram the approval of the bank's charter through the confederation. Thomas Willing was president of the new central bank. Alexander Hamilton, Robert Morse, and Thomas Willing were also behind the Bank of North America. The new central bank was called the First Bank of America. Nothing had changed except the name.

Chapter 17

The Constitutional Convention

Thomas Jefferson stated, "If the American people ever allowed private banks to control the issue of their currency, first by inflation, then by deflation, the banks and the corporations which grow up around them will deprive the people of all their property until their children wake up homeless on the continent their fathers conquered."

Governor Morris represented the state of Pennsylvania at the Constitutional Convention. He stated, "The rich will strive to establish their domination and enslave the rest. They always did and they always will. They will have the same effect here as elsewhere, if we do not, by the power of government, keep them in their proper spheres."

Chapter 18

The First Bank of America

Hamilton and Morse convinced constitutional leaders *not* to give to the government the power to issue money. The colonial leaders forgot how well the colonial scrip worked before the war. The Bank of England, however, did not forget. The money changers could not stand to have America printing its own money again and continued to create their own privately owned central bank in America.

The Constitution was silent on this matter. This fatal mistake left the door wide open for the money changers to create a privately owned central bank.

Chapter 19

First Bank of the United States

In 1782, Alexander Hamilton graduated from law school and became an aide to Robert Morse. This got Hamilton in with the international bankers. On July 2, 1787, Hamilton wrote a letter to James Madison regarding the creation of a privately owned central bank.

In 1790, the money changers wasted no time proposing their idea to Alexander Hamilton and the constitutional leaders. In the same year, Mayer Amschel Rothschild stated, "Let me issue and control the money, and I care not who writes the laws."

In 1791, the Constitution passed a bill to give this new bank a twenty-year charter. It was to be called the First Bank of the United States, or BUS for short. This new privately owned central bank was given a monopoly in printing US currency. The US Department of Treasury first issued US currency in 1862. The denominations were one cent, five cents, twenty-five cents, and fifty cents.

The plan was for 80 percent of its shares to be held by private investors, and the government would purchase the other 20 percent. This ruse worked well.

The constitutional leaders thought they were getting a piece of the action. The real con was for the Constitution to *first* put up the *initial capital*. This was the case in the other privately owned central banks that failed. The private investors never paid for the full amount of their shares.

The Constitution put up the initial $2 million in cash. This gave the money changers enough capital to create the additional capital and borrow the money using the *fractional reserve system*. This method was used to create the other $8 million, giving the private owners enough capital to borrow and buy their shares in the bank. This is outright fraud, a felony.

As with the Bank of England, the private investors were never revealed. Many years later, it was discovered that the Rothschilds were the power behind the creation of the central bank of the United States. The money changers told the constitutional leaders that this privately owned central bank was needed to stabilize the economy and eliminate inflation. However, in the first five years after the central bank was created, the government borrowed $8.2 million—and prices rose by 72 percent.

Chapter 20

Napoleon's Rise to Power

The privately owned central bank of France was also modeled after the privately owned central bank of England. Napoleon never trusted the bank. He said that whenever the bank lent the government money, the bank was the one in control. He also stated, "The hand that gives is above the hand that takes. Money has no motherland; financiers are without patriotism and without decency: their sole object is gain."

In 1800, Thomas Jefferson narrowly defeated John Adams to become the third president of the United States. In 1803, Jefferson and Napoleon made a deal. The US gave Napoleon $3 million in gold for a chunk of land west of the Mississippi River. This came to be known as the Louisiana Purchase.

With the gold, Napoleon forged an army and set across Europe, conquering everything in his path. However, the Bank of England quickly rose to oppose him. They feared that Napoleon would conquer England as well. The Bank of England financed all of the armies in his path as well, reaping enormous profits from the wars.

Prussia, Austria, and Russia went deeply into debt while trying to stop Napoleon. Four years later, thirty-year-old Nathan Rothschild personally took charge of a bold plan to smuggle a much-needed shipment of gold right through France to finance an attack by the Duke of Wellington of Spain. This was, for him, a good business plan. It would keep the war going—and the loan interest payments continuing. Wellington defeated Napoleon and forced him to abdicate. Louis VXIII was crowned king.

Napoleon was exiled to a small island, Elba, off the coast of Italy in 1814. He escaped and was hunted down by the French army. However, he had such charisma and leadership that the army joined him and hailed him as their leader. In 1815, Napoleon was defeated in thc Battle of Waterloo.

Chapter 21

Death of the Bank of the United States

In 1811, the Constitution put forth a bill in renewing the charter of the new Bank of the United States. The bill was defeated. The legislators from Pennsylvania and Virginia passed a resolution to create a new central bank. The press openly attacked the new central bank, calling it a lender, a vulture, and so on.

Congressman T. V. Porter attacked the central bank from the floor of the Constitution, stating, "If this bank's charter was renewed, it would plant a viper on the bosom of this land. It would sting the liberties of this land to the heart."

It did not look good for the new central bank. However, the Rothschilds warned the United States that if the charter was not renewed, they would find themselves in a devastating war. The bill was defeated by a single vote in the House of Representatives. By then, James Madison was in the White House. He was a staunch opponent of the bank. The Senate was in a dead tie to renew the bank's charter. Vice President George Clinton broke the tie and sent the privately owned central bank into *oblivion*.

Within five months, England attacked the US, just as the Rothschilds had threatened, and the War of 1812 began. However, the British were still fighting Napoleon, and the War of 1812 ended in a draw in 1814. Even though the money changers were down, they were far from out. It would take them only three years to bring back their privately owned central bank. It would be bigger and stronger than ever.

Chapter 22

Napoleon and Waterloo

Napoleon rose rapidly through the ranks during the French Revolution. After a disastrous invasion of Russia in 1812, Napoleon abdicated the throne. Two years later he was exiled to the Island of Elba off the coast of Italy. In 1815, he briefly came back to power and suffered a crushing defeat at Waterloo and again abdicated and exiled to the remote island of St. Helena where he died at age fifty-one.

After Waterloo, it was clearly demonstrated how cunning the Rothschilds were in taking over the Bank of England.

Why finance both sides? War offers the biggest profits of all possible business ventures. It wasn't unusual to lend to both sides in a conflict. The evil Rothschilds could not lose. They would get their interest no matter who won the war. It was noted in both loans that the victor would honor the debt to the bankers from both countries.

At Waterloo, thousands of British and French troops gave their lives on a hot summer day.

Nathan Rothschild used the war to take over the Bank of England. A trusted agent of the Rothschilds took off for England to tell Nathan that if Wellington lost and Napoleon won, it would bode ill for England. Nathan took his position in the stock exchange floor, looked very sad, and started to sell his positions. The others started to liquidate their positions, thinking that Napoleon had won and certain financial situations would become perilous. When the stock market crashed, Nathan silently bought bonds and gold coins for a small fraction of their worth.

In just a matter of hours, Nathan dominated the stock market and the Bank of England. One hundred years later, *The New York Times* revealed what had really happened. A grandson of the Rothschilds was sued and lost. The family was ordered by the courts to pay all of the court costs. It took a century, but the family's cunning caught up with them.

Chapter 23

Second Bank of the United States

In 1816, Congress passed a resolution to create another privately owned central bank after the previous ones failed to be created. It was called the Second Bank of the United States. Later, it was called BUS. Again, it would give the government a 20 percent share. The government would put up its share immediately.

This reserve was used to borrow money to lend to the investors for buying the remaining shares using the *fractional reserve system.* Just as before, the primary shareholders remained a secret. It was stated in financial circles that the Rothschilds took over the Bank of England and the Second Bank of the United States as well.

Apparently, the Rothschilds will never give up in establishing a privately owned central bank in the US. The Rothschilds are bankers, and bankers have a lot of money to bribe our constitutional leaders. The Rothschilds will go to any lengths to establish the bank because they want to control our economy and issuance of our money. Many of our elected officials have gone along with Congress in establishing a privately owned central bank.

We are fortunate to have an opposing powerful force in the Tea Party. We must join them to create an even more powerful force in opposing these bribed elected officials.

CHAPTER 24

PRESIDENT ANDREW JACKSON

After twelve years of manipulation the American people could take no more. To the surprise of the Rothschilds, Andrew Jackson was elected in 1828. He wasted no time in opposing the central bank. However, the central bank's charter did not come up for renewal till 1836. Andrew Jackson came up for reelection in 1832. The bankers struck an early blow. The bankers bribed the constitutional leaders into passing a renewal of the charter four years early. Andrew Jackson did not sign the bill and stated quote.

"It is not our citizens only who are to receive the bounty of our government. More than $8 million of this bank are held by foreigners … is there no danger to our liberty or independence in a bank that in its nature has so little to bind it to our country? Controlling our currency, receiving our public money, and holding thousands of our citizens in dependence would be more formidable and dangerous than a military power of the enemy.

If the government could confine itself to equal protection and as heaven does its rains, showers its favors alike on the high and the low, the rich and the poor, it would be an unqualified blessing. In the act before me there seems to be a wide and unnecessary departure for these just principles".

Without question, President Jackson knew exactly what was going on, and he was not about to let it happen or be bribed. President Jackson knew the dangers of a privately owned central bank that would have full control of our economy, money, and our banks.

Later in that year, the Constitution was unable to override Jackson's veto. He stood maybe not to be reelected. For the first time in American history, he took his campaign on the road to the people. Before then, presidential candidates stood at Constitution Hall in Pennsylvania.

The central bank gave more than $3 million to his opposition, Pace. However, Jackson won in a landslide. Jackson knew the battle was only beginning. President Jackson ordered his secretary of Treasury, Louis McCain, to start removing the government deposits of the Second US Bank to safe banks.

McCain refused to do so, and Jackson fired him. Jackson then appointed William J. Bryan as the new Secretary of Treasury. He also refused to do so, and Jackson fired him as well. He then appointed Roger D. Paine for the office. On October 1, 1832, Secretary Paine started to remove the US deposits. Finally, a great president who knew what was going on put a stop to the central US Bank.

Nicholas Biddle of the American Banking Association stated, "This worthy president thinks because he scalped Indians and imprisoned judges, he is to have his way with the bank, he is mistaken." Biddle also said the bank would make the money scarce to force the constitution to restore the bank. Biddle "Nothing but widespread suffering will produce any effect on the constiturion--- our only safety is in pursuing a steady course of firm restriction and I have no doubt that such a course will ultimately lead to restoration of the currency and the re-charter of the bank." He used the power of the bank to cause a massive depression, causing the American people to give in.

Biddle made good on his threat by calling in all loans and not renewing any credit. A financial panic ensued, which was followed by a deep economic depression. Biddle blamed Andrew Jackson, stating the withdrawal of deposits from the central bank. Newspaper articles blasted Jackson in editorials. Jackson was then censored by the Constitution with a vote of twenty-six to twenty. It was the first time that a president was censored.

Jackson lashed out at the central bank. Quote "You are a viper and I intend to wipe you out and by God I will wipe you out". The Constitution was about to renew the central bank's charter for twenty years or more. However, the governor of Pennsylvania George Wolf came out supporting the president and opposed the renewal of the central banks charter. The power shifted to the president. In April 1834, the Constitution voted 134 to 82 against renewing the central bank's charter.

This action was followed up by the creation of a constitutional committee to investigate if the central bank had caused the economic crash. It was an even more lopsided vote to do so. This writer is in shock. Finally, the Constitution got it all together. Don't act investigate—and do something about it.

In the meantime, Biddle was caught—in public—stating that he was about to trash the economy. The Constitution, armed with a subpoena, asked Biddle to give them the books. Biddle refused. The committee wanted to know about the loans that Biddle made. Biddle refused to give up the books or testify.

On January 8, 1835, Andrew Jackson paid off the final debt backed by the currency. He used cold cash to pay off the debt. This is exactly what our government must do today. Several weeks later, on January 30, 1835, Richard Lawrence tried to assassinate the president. Luckily, both pistols misfired. He was tried and found not guilty by reason of insanity.

Lawrence bragged after his release that the international bankers put him up to the task and would defect him if caught. An evil one confesses, and the truth is revealed. In the third year when the Central Bank of the US charter ended, it would cease to function. Biddle was later arrested and charged with fraud. He was tried and acquitted. It appears to me that we have to work on our incompetent court system. However, Biddle was sued and tied up in civil suits.

After Jackson's second term, he retired to Nashville Tennessee. He was remembered as the president who killed the central bank. As a matter of fact, he did so well that he killed the central bank for seventy-seven years.

Chapter 25

Abe Lincoln's Presidency

Although Jackson killed the central bank, the most devastating weapon remained in use—the *fractional reserve system.* The economy thrived and moved westward. The money changers struggled to maintain their position in central banking. They went back to the old formula and created war, debt, and dependency. The Rothschilds would plunge the US in a war just as was done with England and France. In 1812, the First Bank of the US was not re-chartered. The Rothschilds controlled this privately owned bank.

On April 12, 1861, Abe Lincoln knew that the war depended upon slavery. He had no intention of eliminating it. The North received large excise taxes from the slave trade. Only one month after his inaugural address, Lincoln said, "I have no purpose, directly or indirectly, to interfere with the institution of slavery in the states where it now exists. I believe I have no lawful right to do so." He continued to insist that the war was not about slavery. He further stated, "My paramount objective is to save the union and it is not to save or destroy slavery. If I could save the union without freeing any slave, I would do it." source: many documents by lincoln's library.

Lincoln's Emancipation Proclamation was issued on January 1, 1863. However, it took several years to free most of the slaves while the North took control. Moreover, the Emancipation Proclamation did not apply to the five slave states that were not in rebellion or to most regions controlled by the Union.

Emancipation would come after separate state actions and after the December 1865 ratification of the thirteenth amendment, which made slavery illegal. The Emancipation Proclamation did not outlaw slavery and did not make the freed slaves citizens.

On September 22, 1862 Lincoln issued a preliminary proclamation that ordered all slaves in any of the Confederate states of America that did not return to Union control by January 1, 1863, none returned, and the order signed on January 1, 1863, took effect, except in locations where the Union had already regained control.

John Wilkes Booth, an actor, shot Lincoln on April 14, 1865. Lincoln died the next morning. Booth killed Lincoln because he was angry that Lincoln supported voting rights for former slaves. The war was coming to an end. Booth was chased by the American soldiers and killed at a farm in Virginia twelve days after the assassination. Booth became politically active in the 1850s joining the Know Nothing Party. This group wanted fewer immigrants to come to the US. Booth strongly supported slavery in 1859. During the Civil

War, Booth worked as a Confederate secret agent. Booth met frequently with the heads of the Secret Service—Jacob Thompson and Clement Clay—in Montreal. Booth's plot to kidnap Lincoln in the summer of 1864 failed. In March 1865, Booth attended Lincoln's second inauguration.

Booth and his fellow conspirators met at a restaurant three blocks from Ford Theatre to plan the kidnapping. Some coconspirators dismissed the plan as unworkable. After the fall of the Confederate capital at Richmond on April 4 and General Lee's large-scale surrender on April 9, Booth decided to assassinate Lincoln.

Before then, the money changers saw an opportunity to start a war between the North and the South. This would weaken the US. The money changers concocted a wild conspiracy scheme. However, Otto Von Bismarck, the chancellor of Germany stated, "The division of the United States into federations of equal force was decided long before the Civil War by the high financial powers of Europe. These bankers were afraid that the United States, if they remained as one block and as one nation, would attain economic and financial independence, which would upset their financial domination over the world's currency." source, wikipedia/google

The money changers were anxious to see the Union fail and offered loans at 24 to 36 percent. Lincoln said thanks, but no thanks and returned to Pennsylvania. He then turned to an old friend, Colonel Dick Taylor, and put him on the problem of financing the war. During one meeting, he asked Taylor what he found out. Taylor said, "Why, Lincoln, that's easy; just get constitution to pass a bill authorizing the printing of full *legal tender* treasury notes and pay your soldiers and suppliers of war material and go ahead and win your war. Abe Lincoln said what will the American people think about this.

Taylor replied, "The people or anyone else would not have any choice in the matter, if you made them full *legal tender.* The notes will have the full sanction of the government and be just as good as any money; the Constitution had given that express right." This is exactly what Lincoln did.

In 1862 and 1863, Lincoln authorized the Constitution to print $450 million of the new bills. One problem was making a distinction from the existing script. Lincoln used green ink on the backside. They were later called greenbacks. With this money, he paid the troops and suppliers of war materials. The greenbacks resulted in no interest to the central government. Lincoln knew who was pulling the strings and what was at stake for the American people.

Lincoln stated: Quote "The government should create, issue, and circulate all the currency and credit needed to satisfy the spending power of the government and the buying power of consumers. The privilege of issuing money is not only the supreme prerogative of government, but is the government's greatest creative opportunity. By the adoption of these principles the taxpayers will be saved immense sums of interest. Money will cease to the master and become the servant of humanity". source: Lincoln's library of statements and records

Lincoln did not consider the destructive force of inflation. Spending this huge amount of money and then issuing bonds (debt) is a serious inflation problem. Currently the feds sell treasury bills and treasury notes every week and treasury bonds each month, without a provision for paying it back.

In 1863, the North and South troops amassed for the decisive battle of the Civil War. The needs for additional money grew. Lincoln pushed through the National Bank Act. The banks would buy government bonds and hold them as a reserve against the greenbacks. The banks would pay no taxes on the interest they received. From that point on, the government would operate in debt.

John K. Galbraith, the economist said, "The numerous years following the war, the federal government ran a heavy surplus. It could not however, pay off its debt, or retire its securities, because to do so, there would be no bonds to back the national bank notes, to pay off the debt was to destroy the money supply."

I disagree with Galbraith 100 percent. Backing is sheer nonsense because of the good faith of the government. We know the government is not going out of business. The government first pays off the debt (just as Jackson did), and then it retires its securities. The banks have no say in the matter.

Later in 1863, Lincoln got some unexpected help from the czar of Russia. Alexander II and Otto Von Bismarck both knew what the money changers were up to. A central bank was set up in Russia. If America survived the Civil War, the czar's position would remain secure. Greenbacks would continue to circulate—but would not be increased. This decision not to increase the greenbacks became known as the Contracting Act of April 12, 1866. The Rothschilds knew that more money was needed for the Civil War and after the war. America would have to create money or borrow heavily from the Rothschilds.

Russia and the US would then be under the control of the central banks and would threaten Russia again into borrowing heavily from the Rothschild. However, if England or France intervened, Russia and the US would consider it a declaration of war. Lincoln was reelected in 1864. He said, "The money power prays upon the nation in times of peace and conspires against it in times of adversity. It is more despotic than monarchy, more insolent than autocracy, more selfish than bureaucracy."

After Lincoln's assassination, Salmon P. Chase said, "My agency in promoting the passage of the National Banking Act was the greatest financial mistake in my life. It has built up a monopoly which affects every interest in the country." source: wikipedia/google research Allegations of the international bankers causing the death of Lincoln surfaced seventy years later in 1934. Canadian Gerry McGeer had a four-point plan that included a national bank, a credit control tax, an internal trade department, and a foreign exchange office. McGeer proved his allegations of the international bankers involvement in the assassination of Lincoln in May of 1934 in the newspapers.

The international bankers wanted to stop the greenbacks and put America on a gold standard, which they controlled. Lincoln did the opposite by issuing the greenbacks solely on the credit and good faith of the US government. The notes were issued every year till 1953.

In 1954, the greenbacks went out of circulation and were replaced by the new notes. This was bad news for the international bankers because silver was plentiful and gold was scarce and could easily be controlled. At one time, only 261 million ounces of gold was mined *in the entire world.* Historically, silver is fifteen times more plentiful.

Chapter 26

The Return of the Gold Standard

With the opening of the West, silver was discovered in huge quantities. The greenbacks were still popular; despite the constant attack by the international bankers, they continued to circulate.

W. Cleon Skousen said, "Right after the Civil War, there was considerable talk about reviving Lincoln's brief experiment with the constitutional monetary system. Had the European money trust not intervened, it would no doubt become an established institution." source: wikipedia/google research. This sent shockwaves throughout the central bankers in Europe. On April 12, 1866—nearly one year to the day after Lincoln's death—the central bank passed the Contracting Act, authorizing the Treasury to retire the greenbacks and thereby the money supply.

Why did Congress pass such an act? This act served no other purpose than to cause an economic depression. Could it be that some committee heads were bribed? What about the others on the committee who were not bribed? Did the committee heads put stupid dolts on the committee that could easily be manipulated? If this is the case, we must vote them all out of office since they would not be qualified to run for office.

Now the deadliest act of them all was passed on December 23, 1913. The Federal Reserve Act of 1913 was passed in the wee hours of the morning. Only three senators were present in Congress; the rest had been told to go home for the holiday recess because nothing would be done till they got back. That made this legislation illegal among other actions.

The money changers wanted two things: a privately owned central bank and a monetary system backed by gold. The money changers created a series of panics to convince the American people that centralized control was the only answer to stability. This act would make the American people so poor they wouldn't care or to weak to oppose the bankers. Here is what happened next.

Post Civil War Depression

Year	Total Dollars	Per Capita
1866	1,800,000,000	$50.46
1867	1,300,000,000	$44.00
1876	600,000,000	$14.60
1886	400,000,000	$6.67

At that point two-thirds of the money supply had been called in by the central bank. The jerks in the constitution allowed the bankers to do this while our population grew. This resulted in a 750 percent loss of buying power in twenty years. The economists called this an up-and-down business cycle. Obviously, they had no clue about what was really happening as is the case today. Loans were called in, and no new loans were given. The silver coins were melted down. This left the population without any money.

In 1872, the Central Bank of England gave Ernest Seyd 100,000 pounds—about $500,000. He went to America to bribe the necessary congressmen to get silver demonetized. Seyd, a German banker living in England was an expert in coinage. Seyd was told to draw more money if necessary. In the very next year, Congress passed the *Coin Act,* stating that Seyd actually drafted the legislation. This was a boldfaced lie because only legislators could draft legislation—and it had to be done in the Constitution Hall.

In 1874, Seyd admitted who was behind the scheme. He said, "I went to America in the winter of 1872–1873, authorized to secure the passage of a bill demonetizing silver. It was in the interest of those I represented, the governors of the Bank of England to have it done." source: wikipedia/google research. This writer does not care who or how it was passed. I rarely vote for any incumbent to be elected. Voters who reelect them deserve their own grief.

In 1873, gold coins were the only form of coin money. The control of America's money was not over. Only three years later, one-third of America's workforce was unemployed—and the population was growing restless. The people demanded the return of the greenbacks, silver coins, or anything that would make money more plentiful.

That year, the constitution created a silver commission to study the problem. The US Silver Commission's report clearly blamed the money contraction on the international bankers. The report stated that decreasing the money supply and falling prices created the disaster of the Dark Ages. Without money, civilization could not have had a beginning. And with a diminishing supply, it must languish and unless relieved, finally perish. No solution here but true. We paid the committee for nothing, which is the case today.

In the Christian Era, the metallic money of the Roman Empire amounted to 1.8 billion; by the end of the fifteenth century it had shrunk to less than 200 million. *History records no other disastrous transition* as that from the Roman Empire to the late Middle Ages. Note: The figures represent the purchasing power of that time period.

Moreover, the excessive spending of public works in that era caused the decrease in purchasing power. The substantial reduction of money to the people at that time caused the depression.

The Constitution took no action on this report. In April 1877, riots broke out in Pittsburgh, Ohio, and Chicago. The international bankers decided to hang on. The bankers convinced Congress to retire the greenbacks.

In a letter to the constitution it said, "it is advisable to do all in your power to sustain the religious press as will oppose the greenback issue of paper money and that you will also hold patronage from all applicants who are not willing to oppose the government issue of money.

To repeal the act creating banknotes, to restore to circulation the government issue of money, will be to provide the people with money. This would seriously affect our individual profits as bankers and lenders. See your congressman at once. Tell him or her to support our interests that we may control legislation, James Buel American Bankers Association.

Why did Buel get this brazen? The constitutional leaders let him get away with it. The people in those days had all they could do just to make a dollar for the bare necessities leave alone vote.

On January 8, 1878, the *New York Tribune* stated, "The capital of this country is well organized at last and will see if the constitution dare fly in its face." However, it didn't work that well. On February 28, 1878, congress passed the Sherman Act, ending the five-year hiatus. The act limited the number of silver dollars in circulation. Prior to 1873, anyone could have silver coins stamped into silver dollars for free. The Sherman Act stopped this practice. Some money now flowed back into the economy, and no further threat appeared to the money changers.

James Garfield was elected president in 1881 and knew what was going on. In his inaugural address, he said, "Whosoever controls the volume in any country is absolute master of all industry and commerce. When you realize that the entire system is very easily controlled one way or the other, by a few powerful men at the top, you will not have to be told how periods of inflation and depression originate." source: wikipedia/ google research.

Sadly, a few weeks after his address, on July 2, 1881, he was assassinated. Could it have been the international bankers at it again?

CHAPTER 27

FREE SILVER

The money changers will still create booms and busts to buy farms and land for pennies on the dollar and then make loans for the full value of the land or farms. In 1891, the money changers were set to start an economic depression. Here we go again. A letter from the American Bankers Association to Congress made this absolutely clear.

We will start a depression in thirty days from now three years in the future. On September 1, 1894 we will not renew our loans under any considerations. On September 1, we will demand our money. We will foreclose and become mortgagees in possession. We can take two thirds of the farms west of the Mississippi and thousands of them east of the Mississippi, at our own price. The farmers will become tenants as it was in England.

In 1891, American Bankers Association as printed in the, mind you, congressional record of April 29, 1913. Did congress warn us of this total disaster? No. Why not? Did the people pay attention? No. They just wanted their silver money restored. Revolting, they called the sad act of 73 the crime act of 73. The Fourth Coinage Act of 1873 demonetized silver coins and reduced that type of money at that time to cause an economic depression.

In 1896, silver had become the central issue of the presidential campaign. William Jennings Bryan gave a powerful speech ever made in a political convention. Only thirty-six at the time, he said, "We will answer their demands for a gold standard by saying to them: you shall not press down upon the brow of labor this crown of thorns, you shall not crucify mankind upon a cross of gold." Thus began the most fiercely contested presidential race in American history. The money changers blasted Bryan and succeeded; McKinley won the race by a small margin.

In 1912, Bryan was appointed Secretary of State in the Woodrow Wilson administration. He served only two years before resigning in 1915 over the highly suspicious sinking of the *Lusitania*. Twenty-six Americans were killed on the British ocean liner, driving America into World War I. However, Bryan's efforts delayed the money changers' goals for seventeen years.

Chapter 28

J.P. Morgan and the 1907 Crash

The Aldrich bill was condemned in the platform when Woodrow Wilson was nominated. The men who ruled the democratic party promised the people that if they returned to power there would be no central bank while they were in power. They never meant what they said. Once in power, they would go ahead with the privately owned central bank. Blindly, the democratic voters vote party and do not analyze what is going on to their detriment. The Democratic party were liars then as they always have been in history.

In 1902, Theodore Roosevelt enforced the Sherman Antitrust Act of 1890. This act was created to break up monopolies. It was thought that President Teddy Roosevelt broke up the Standard Oil Company monopoly. However, it was only broken up into seven smaller corporations and still owned and controlled by John D. Rockefeller.

In 1907, Morgan pushed to start a new privately owned central bank. Morgan and his friends secretly conspired to crash the stock market. He deported thousands of foreign banks. In addition, he created rumors that a major bank was to collapse. A run followed on that bank and others. This started a stock market crash. He had full control of the American banks. With the fractional reserve system, he was able to create money out of nothing.

Morgan's proposal to Congress was far worse than the fractional reserve system, but Congress let him do it. It is incredible that the people we put in office to represent us will destroy us. With a green light from Congress, Morgan manufactured $300 million of worthless money. He loaned some of it to his friends and cronies at interest. His plan worked; as the public gained confidence, it started to use the money.

Woodrow Wilson said, "All this trouble could be averted if we appointed a committee of six or seven public-spirited men like J. P. Morgan to handle the affairs of our country." The stupid Wilson later ate his words and apologized to the American people when he found out what Morgan had done.

In 1923, Charles A. Lindbergh said, "That the panic of 1907 was an outright sham. It was used later to create taxation and the Federal Reserve System in 1913." He also stated, "Those not favorable to the money-trust could be squeezed out of business and the people frightened into demanding changes in the banking and currency laws which the money trust would then frame."

Chapter 29

The Secret of Jekyll Island

A series of booms and busts followed. Property would be seized for pennies on the dollar. These evil shams convinced people that a central bank was needed to stabilize the country. After the 1907 crash, Teddy Roosevelt created a commission to study the cause of the crash in response to the people's demands. Naturally, the commission was loaded with Morgan's cronies and friends.

The chairman was Senator Nelson Aldrich. He represented the richest banking families in America. One of them was John D. Rockefeller. John D. Rockefeller had five sons: John, Nelson, Lawrence, Winthrop, and David. Nelson later became the chairman and head of Chase Manhattan Bank. Paul Warburg, a naturalized German citizen, had his Manhattan bank merge with Rockefeller's Chase Bank, making it the Chase Manhattan Bank.

Senator Aldrich went on a two-year tour of Europe, costing the taxpayers $300,000. This was a huge sum at that time. Aldrich consulted at length with the Central Bank of England and the central banks of Germany and France. These privately owned central banks were created and controlled by the Rothschilds. Shortly after

Aldrich's return, on November 22, 1910, some of the wealthiest bankers in America boarded his private rail car. In the strictest secrecy, they went to Jekyll Island to create illegal legislation that was designed to control our banking system and our economy.

Paul Warburg was with them. Paul Warburg was born in Germany, married an American and became a US citizen. Warburg was given a salary of $500,000 per year to lobby and bribe for a privately owned central bank in America.

The Rothschilds, Schiffs, and Warburgs all were interrelated by marriage through the years. In the US, the Rockefellers, Morgans, and Aldriches were also interrelated by marriage.

Secrecy was so tight that all were cautioned to use only their first names so that the servants will not know their identities.

Frank Vanderlip was to head the First National Bank in New York City. I was as secretive, in deed as furtive as any conspirator. Discovery we knew must not happen or else all our time and effort would be wasted. If it were to be exposed that our particular group had got together and written a banking bill, that bill would have no chance of passage in Congress. This confession is irrefutable proof that the Federal Reserve System and the IRS created in 1913 is 100 percent illegal. I rest my case on this confession alone. Warburg and the others knew that legislation had to be conducted in Congress by legislators only. Most importantly, two thirds of both houses had to be assembled to create any legislation according to the Constitution.

On Jekyll Island, they conspired on how to create a privately owned central bank. The market share of the big banks was sinking fast. In the first decade of the twentieth century, the number of banks doubled to more than 20,000. By 1913, 29 percent were national banks—and they held 57 percent of all deposits.

In a newspaper article, Senator Aldrich admitted, "Before passage of this act, the New York bankers could only dominate the reserves of New York. Now we are able to dominate the bank reserves of the entire country. John D. Rockefeller said, "Competition is sin".

However, the economy got so strong that corporations were able to finance their expansion through their corporate profits. In the first decade of the twentieth century, about 70 percent came from corporate profits without borrowing.

Corporations had become independent of the money changers, and that had to be stopped. Aldrich's ego got to him, and he insisted that the bill be named after him.

After nine days, it was settled. The new central bank would be similar to the old Bank of the US. It would be given a monopoly over banks and create money *out of nothing*. The government would issue bonds and pay interest on it. At the end of ten years, the principal would be paid off—and the bond ended. There were 3.6 trillion of these bonds at that time. We see how our debt started, and now it has expanded to more than $18 trillion.

CHAPTER 30

THE FED'S MONEY-MAKING PROCESS

This is a very critical chapter and must be carefully studied.

1) The Federal Open Market Committee (FOMC) approves the purchase of the US bonds.
2) The US bonds are purchased by the feds from whocver is offering them in the open market.
3) The feds pay for the bonds with electronic credits to the seller's bank. These credits are based on nothing. The feds just create them out of thin air.
4) The banks use these deposits as reserves. The banks then can loan out ten times these reserves to new borrowers (all at interest). The feds create 10 percent of the money, and the banks create the other 90 percent. The feds sell the bonds to the banks, and the money flows out of the banks. For example, a sale of $1 million in bonds to the banks results in $10 million out of the economy.

How do banks benefit from this?

1) Misdirected banking reform.
2) Block the greenbacks from making a comeback.
3) Delegate to the banks to create 90 percent of our money supply based upon the fractional reserve system and loan it out all at interest.
4) Centralize overall control of the nation's money.
5) Establish a central bank with a high degree of independence from effective political control. This gave the feds the power to create the *retraction of money.* This caused the Great Depression. In order to fool our government that they were in control, the plan called for seven governors to be appointed by the president and approved by the Senate.

All the bankers had to do was to make sure their men got to be appointed to the board of governors. This was easy. The bankers had money—and money bought influence in politics. The subterfuge did not work. The Aldrich Bill was quickly identified as the Central Bankers' Bill. This became known as the *money trust.*

Charles A. Lindbergh stated, "The Aldrich bill is the Wall Street plan. It means another panic, if necessary, to intimidate the people."

Aldrich—who was paid by the government to represent the people—proposed a plan for the trust instead. Republican leaders never brought the bill to a vote because they didn't have enough votes to win. The central bankers decided to use their plan a Democratic alternative.

The central bankers would finance Woodrow Wilson as the Democratic nominee. Wilson received an indoctrination course from the Democratic leaders convened there.

CHAPTER 31

THE FEDERAL RESERVE ACT OF 1913

Pennsylvania Representative Louis T. McFadden said, "Established here in our free country is a worm-eating monarchial institution of the king's bank to control from the top downward and to shackle us from the cradle to the grave." source: congressional records.

Once Wilson was elected in 1913, Morgan, Warburg, Baruch, and others created a new plan, which they called the Federal Reserve System. The Democratic leadership hailed the new bill, which they called the Glass-Owens Bill. The Democratic leadership also stated that the bill was very different, but it was identical to the Aldrich Bill. Paul Warburg, the creator of both bills, stopped the Democratic argument and advised his paid friends in Congress that both bills were identical. He said, "Brushing aside the external differences affecting the shells, we find the kernels of the two systems very closely resembled and related to one another." source: congressional records.

In one of the Jekyll Island meetings, Frank Vanderlip, president of the First National Bank, opposed the plan. Years later, Vanderlip admitted in the *Saturday*

Evening Post that both bills were virtually the same. He stated, "Although the Aldrich Federal Reserve plan was defeated when it bore the name Aldrich, its essential points were all contained in the bill (Glass-Owens) that was finally adopted."

Another admission by one involved proves my point again about the illegality of the feds and the IRS in the Federal Reserve Act of 1913.

The argument continued, and Congress hired an attorney to explain both bills. Alfred Crozier from Ohio said, "The bill grants just what Wall Street and the big banks for twenty years have been striving for, private instead of public control of currency."

The Glass-Owen Bill does this as completely as the Aldrich bill. Both measures rob the government and the people of effective control over the public money vested in the banks exclusively, the dangerous power to make money among the people scarce or plentiful. The senators complained that the big banks were using their influence to gain an advantage. Despite the charges of deceit and corruption, the bill was pushed through the Senate on December 22, 1915. Actually, it was done in the wee hours of December 23. The treasonous Senator Nelson Aldrich died on April 16, 1915, in New York City. Obviously, others were involved and bribed that took Aldrich's place.

Here's how it was done. The bribed leadership reassured the senators that nothing would be done till they reconvened after the holidays. Let us go to the language in the sixteenth amendment as proposed by

Congress. The sixteenth amendment to the United States Constitution adds a federal income tax.

Passed by Congress on July 2, 1909, and ratified on February 3, 1913, the sixteenth amendment established Congress's right to impose a federal income tax. The next language is extremely important and deserves to be read at least three times till it sinks in.

> Article XV1: The Congress shall have the power to lay and collect taxes on incomes, from whatever source derives, without apportionment among the several states, and without regard to any census or enumeration.
>
> Joint Resolution" states specifically that two-thirds of each House must be assembled and concurring therein. That the following article is proposed as an amendment in the Constitution of the United States, which, when ratified by the legislators of three fourths of the several states, shall be valid to all interests to all intents and purposes as a part of the Constitution.

There it is in black and white. The amendment was never legally executed. Many of our laws were also never legally executed.

> On the day the bill was passed, Charles Lindbergh sent a warning to his countrymen:
>
> This act establishes the most gigantic trust on earth. When the president signs

> this bill, the invisible government by the monetary power will be legalized. The people may not know it immediately. But the day of reckoning is only a few years hence. It will be the worst legislative crime of the ages that will be perpetrated by this bill.

Even Lindbergh did not realize the illegal procedure by the senators on December 23, 1915.

The central bankers have in place a system that would create *unlimited debt and have the American people pay for it through the powers given to the IRS.* The interest itself would be huge. The interest would be guaranteed by the people through income taxation. The money changers knew if they raised the interest rate, the people would revolt, not pay the interest, or keep the debt small.

In 1872, the US Supreme Court ruled that income tax was unconstitutional and therefore should be eliminated. In 1895, the Supreme Court ruled that income tax for individuals was unconstitutional. In 1909, the Supreme Court ruled that income tax for corporations was also unconstitutional. Treasonous Senator Aldrich hustled the sixteenth amendment to Congress. The sixteenth amendment would overcome all the confusion involved in defining the income tax controversy.

Congress sent it to the forty-eight states; 75 percent of the forty-eight states had to ratify it. Only twenty two did, and sixteen did not. This meant the sixteenth amendment was never legally carried.

Prior to that time, the war of income taxation had raged for many decades. The Constitution struggled with it in America. Here's how it was bandied about. One constitutional member would say what is the meaning of direct or indirect taxes and how was it be applied? Was it by national population or state population? Were the slaves to be included in the population? If so, would they be given voting rights? Would it be a flat small per capita tax? Would it be a percentage above a certain amount of income? Would it be a graduated tax?

It became a monster for the constitutional members to handle, and the battle raged on for many decades. We now see why the few bribed senators in Congress had to illegally ram the sixteenth amendment through Congress.

In March 1906, David G. Philips wrote an article in *Cosmopolitan.* "The treason of Senator Nelson Aldrich, the head of it all" exposed how he created the bill.

A year after the bill was passed, Charles Lindbergh weighed in again.

> All the federal reserve has to do to cause high prices is to lower the discount rate producing an expansion of credit and a rising stock market; then when businessmen are adjusted to these conditions, it can check prosperity in midstream by arbitrarily raising the interest rate. It can cause the pendulum of a rising or falling

> market to swing back and forth by slight changes in the discount rate. They can also cause violent fluctuations by a greater rate variation. In either case it will posses inside information as to financial conditions and advance knowledge of the coming changes, either up or down.
>
> This is the most dangerous advantage ever placed in the hands of a few by any government that existed. This system is private and conducted for the sole purpose of obtaining the greatest possible profits from the use of other people's money. They know in advance when to create panics to their advantage. They also know when to stop panics. Inflation and deflation work equally as well for the central bankers when they control finance.

Since Lindbergh was not a leader or speaker, Congress did not have to do anything about the situation he depicted. As stated by Rep. Lindbergh we know why we must disband the feds and the IRS. I will address this severe problem in my concluding chapter.

Only one year later, the feds cornered the gold market. Representative Louis T. McFadden chaired the House Banking Committee from 1920 to 1931. McFadden stated, "A super state controlled by international bankers and international industrialists acting together to enslave the world for their own pleasure." source congressional records. What did Congress do about this? Nothing. We must destroy

Congress and restructure it 100 percent. It is called *cleaning house.*

In 1960, Wright Patman, a congressman from Texas, stated, "In the United States today, we in effect have two governments. We have the duly appointed military uncoordinated government in the Federal Reserve System. It operates the money powers, which are reserved to Congress by the Constitution." source: congressional records. Patman was the chairman of the Banking and Currency Committee. Another statement right from the horse's mouth again—and by a Democrat.

Thomas Edison said, "If our nation can issue a dollar bond, it can issue a dollar bill. The element that makes the bond good makes the bill good. The difference between the bond and the bill is that the bond lets money brokers collect twice the amount of the bond and an additional 20 percent. The currency pays nobody but those who contribute directly in some useful way. It is absurd to say that our country can issue $30 million in bonds and not $30 million in currency. Both are promises to pay, but one promise fattens the usurers and the other helps the people." source: congressional records.

They are creating hundreds of embassies to control the world, selling them war materials, getting billions in kickbacks, and killing and mutilating our military youths too. Could this be under the guise of being the leader of the free world? These are career criminals who don't love anybody. Almost all politicians are only interested in two things: staying in power and becoming wealthy.

Only three years after the passage of the Federal Reserve Act of 1913, President Wilson had other thoughts about it.

> We have come to be one of the most ruled and one of the most completely controlled governments in the civilized world. No longer, are we a government by the vote of the majority, but a government by the opinion and duress of a small group of dominant men. Some of the biggest men in the US, in the field of commerce and manufacturing are afraid of something. They know that there is a power somewhere so organized, so complete so pervasive, that they had better not speak above their breath when they speak in condemnation of it.

In 1924, President Wilson said, "I have willingly ruined my government and apologize to the American people." It was too late. The money changers had their privately owned central bank installed in America. The biased media—bought by the top evil central bankers—hailed the passage of the bill as a means to control inflation and the economy. The course of future events has proven that the money changers have controled our money and economy to their advantage.

Chapter 32

World War I

With the system in place, it was time to start a really big war—a world war. What? Are wars started on purpose? We'll see about that. The central banks were only interested in the huge debt it would create and the huge interest payments on the money they would lend to the nations involved in the wars.

The Rothschilds started a world war only one year after the creation of the private central bank. Naturally, the IRS was created at the same time to enforce the taxes the American people would have to pay for the cost of the war.

The Central Bank of England loaned money to England, and the Rothschild Central Bank of France loaned money to the French.

J. P. Morgan was the war material sales agent for both the English and the French, spending $10 million per day. This was Morgan's reward for joining and being funded by the Rothschilds. Salespeople mobbed the Wall Street brokers to get in on the action. It got so bad that guards had to be posted in the banks, on Wall Street, and even at their homes.

Many New York bankers did very well during the war. President Wilson appointed Bernard Baruch to head the US Embassy Board. It looks like Wilson lost his brains again by putting one of the evil schemers in charge. Meanwhile, Baruch and Rockefeller profited $200 million from the war. Some of the other reasons of the war were that the money changers wanted to get back at Lincoln's guard in support of the war. More importantly, Russia was the only country that refused to give into the privately owned central bank scheme.

Three years after the start of World War I in 1914, the Russian Revolution broke out and toppled the Russian czar. The country turned to communism. Jacob Schiff stated from his deathbed that he spent $20 million to defeat the czar. Money came from England to finance the Russian Revolution. Some of the richest men in the world backed communism to destroy capitalism, which made them rich. Did they want to enslave the world using the so-called new world order scheme?

Yes, indeed! Gary Allen, a freelance journalist in California, who majored in history at Stanford said, If one understands that socialism is not sharing-the-wealth program but it is in reality a method to consolidate and control the wealth, then the seeming paradox of super-rich men promoting socialism becomes no paradox at all. Instead it becomes logical even the perfect tool of power-seeking megalomaniacs. Communism, or more accurately, socialism is not a movement of the downtrodden masses, but of the economic elite.

In 1970, W. Cleon Skousen, wrote *The Naked Capitalist.*

> Power from any source tends to create an appetite for more power. It was almost inevitable that the super rich would one day aspire to control the wealth of the whole world. To achieve this, they were perfectly willing to feed the ambition of the power-hungry political conspirators who were committed to the overthrow of all existing governments and the establishment of a central worldwide dictatorship.

Financing the war and contracting the money supply would keep the opposition under control.

Lenin stated, "The state, does not function as we desired, the car does not obey, a man is at the wheel and seems to lead it, but the car does not drive in the desired direction. It moves as another force wishes." Lenin is stating that he runs the country but others control it.

> The course of Russian history has been greatly affected by the operations of international bankers. The soviet government had been given US Treasury money by the Federal Reserve Board through the Chase Manhattan Bank. This was money illegally given by the feds to the Rothschilds to loan to Russia for its war.

The Central Bank of England withdrew money through the Federal Reserve Board and loaned it out at high interest rates to the Soviets. Hold the phone—did we get the interest on that loan, or did the international bankers pocket the interest with some of our bribed leaders?

The Dnieprostroi Dam was built with funds unlawfully taken by the feds in 1932. The purpose was to create hydroelectric power from the Dnieper River in the Ukraine. It was considered the world's largest dam at that time.

Seven decades of communism followed, and of course, huge debt followed as well. Most—if not all—wars are created by evil and powerful men at the top.

CHAPTER 33

THE GREAT DEPRESSION

Shortly after World War I, the money changers political position shifted to controlling the world's governments under a new world order. This was called the *League of Nations.* However, much to the surprise of Warburg and Baruch, the world did not want to lose sovereignty or its borders and decided against it. In addition, the United States would not ratify it. Many other nations did—even though the money came from the United States.

Meanwhile, the American people grew restless about Wilson's policies. In the presidential election of 1920, Warren Harding won in a landslide. President Harding strongly opposed the League of Nations and Bolshevism. President Harding gave the American people awesome prosperity that became known as the Roaring Twenties. This period occurred even though the economy had ten times the debt of the Civil War.

In the twenties, the governor of the New York Federal Reserve Bank, Benjamin Strong, met secretly with the governor of the Bank of England, Mathew B. Norman. Norman was determined to return the Bank of England to its former dominance in world finance.

However, under the reins of Harding and Coolidge, the debt was reduced by 38 percent to $16 billion. This was the greatest percentage drop in American history. In the ensuing presidential election, Harding and Coolidge ran against Governor Cost of Ohio and Franklin D. Roosevelt. FDR had been the assistant secretary of the navy under Wilson.

After Harding's inauguration, he moved quickly to kill the League of Nations scheme. He lowered excise taxes and raised tariffs to record heights. Our forefathers were smiling in their graves about Harding's policies. In his second year in office, Harding took ill on a train ride to the West and died suddenly.

No autopsy was performed. It was believed he died from food poisoning or pneumonia. Coolidge took over as president and continued President Harding's policies. As a result, the economy grew at a very rapid rate. The money changers had to stop this. The only way was to crash the economy. The Federal Reserve Board began to flood the economy with money, which increased the money by a whooping 62 percent.

Before President Roosevelt's death in 1919, he warned the American people about what was happening. An editorial in the *New York Times* on March 27, 1922 noted what Teddy Roosevelt said, "These international bankers and Rockefeller's Standard Oil Company interests control the majority of newspapers and columns of these papers to club into submission or drive out of public office officials who refuse to do the bidding of the powerful corrupt clique, which is the invisible government."

Only one day before Mayor John Harlan quoted Roosevelt and blasted those he thought was taking control of America, its political elements, and the press. The warning of Theodore Roosevelt has much timeliness today. The real menace of our republic is this invisible government, which like a giant octopus sprawls its slimy length over city, state, and nation. It seizes in its long and powerful tentacles our executive offices, our legislative bodies, our schools, our courts, our newspapers, and every agency created for the public protection.

> They virtually run the US government for their own selfish purposes. They practically run both parties, write political platforms, make cat's paws of party leaders, use the leading men of private organizations and resort to every device to place in nomination for high public office only such candidates as will be amenable to the dictates of corrupt big business.

Wow, I could not have stated it better myself. We must reconstruct Congress in its entirety. *The New York Times* on March 26, 1922, quoted Teddy Roosevelt as saying, "Why did none of the American people balked at this".

No one wants to discuss this in good economic times. More importantly, there were no careers or education in those days. People just struggled to pay the rent and eat.

The money changers expanded credit, and the stock market soared. There were no laws regulating securities. The securities regulations in 1933 and 1934 came after the stock market in 1929. One of the major aspects in the crash was that margin was at 10 percent, which meant people could buy one dollar of securities for only ten cents. When the twenty-four-hour stockbroker margin calls came, no one had the money to cover the calls. This caused the stock market to crash even faster because portfolios were liquidated left and right—at any price. Panic set in, and most lost everything.

Six months after the crash on April 30, 1930, the nation's banks closed their doors. Months later, when the banks opened their doors, the people were so frightened that almost all withdrew their money and warned the clerks that they would not see their faces again.

The money was put in shoe boxes and hidden in attics or buried in tin cans in the back yard. Very little money was in circulation in the entire country, and everything collapsed.

Noted economist John K. Galbraith said, "At the height of the panic selling, Bernard Baruch brought Winston Churchill into the visitor's gallery to watch the stock market crash that he and others created."

Louis T. McFadden was on the banking committee, and he knew who was to blame. "It was not accidental; it was a carefully contrived occurrence. The international bankers sought to bring about a condition of despair so that they might emerge as rulers of us all." He also directly accused them of causing the crash to steal America's gold. In February of 1931, in the midst of the Depression, he said, "I think it can hardly be disputed that the statesmen and financiers of Europe are ready to take any means to reacquire rapidly the gold that Europe lost to America in World War I."

Curtis Dall was the son-in-law of FDR. He was on the New York Stock Exchange floor during the crash. He was a stockbroker with Lehman Brothers. In his 1970 book, he stated, "Actually, it was the calculated shearing of the public by the world money-powers triggered by planned sudden shortage of call money in the New York money market." Within a year, $40 billion vanished—or was it consolidated in fewer hands? These happenings don't just occur—they are caused. If we don't kill the root, the weed will grow again.

The feds could have lowered interest rates to stimulate the economy. However, they chose to contract the money, causing an even steeper economic depression. Between 1929 and 1933, the feds contracted the money supply by an additional 33 percent.

However, the Nobel Prize-winning economist Milton J. Friedman knew what happened. He stated that he agreed with McFadden during a public radio interview in 1996.

> The Federal Reserve definitely caused the Great Depression by contracting the amount of currency in circulation by

> one-third from 1929 to 1933. This reduced wealth was redistributed to the few hands that caused the crash as they had inside knowledge of it and pulled out their shares before the crash and put it in gold and cash. At the same time, money was taken out of the economy while Americans were starving and sent to Germany to rebuild its economy after World War I.

Congress must be completely restructured because we can't have too much power in so few hands.

McFadden warned Americans that our money was being used to bring Hitler to power. After World War I, Germany fell into the German international banker's control. These bankers bought Germany and now own her, lock, stock, and barrel. They have purchased her industry, mortgaged her soil, controlled their production, and control her public utilities. They have subsidized the government of Germany and they have also supplied every dollar that Hitler has used to his campaign to build a threat to the government of Brüning. When Heinrich Brüning fails to obey the orders of the German international bankers, Hitler is brought forth to scare the German people into submission.

Heinrich Brüning was a chancellor and foreign minister of Germany. The feds pumped more than $30 billion of American money into Germany. The Germans used the money to build modern dwellings, planetariums, gymnasiums, swimming pools, and ultrafine public highways—all with our money. The feds pumped so many billions of dollars into Germany that they never mentioned the grand total to the American people.

In 1932, FDR was easily elected as president. He enacted a sweeping banking bill. Unfortunately, it only increased the Fed's power over our money supply. With this increased power, the Fed finally pumped money into the economy for the starving American people. This was the deal that FDR made with the international bankers.

CHAPTER 34

FDR AND WORLD WAR II

In FDR'S inaugural address on March 4, 1933, he said, "Practices of the unscrupulous money changers stand indicted in the court of public opinion, rejected by the hearts and minds of men. The money changers have fled from their seats in the temple of our civilization."

Whenever, politicians orate like this, it is a con job for us. Nothing will be done as was the case before. On April 30, 1930, Roosevelt declared a holiday and closed all the nation's banks. FDR outlawed private ownership of all gold bullion and gold coins with the exception of rare gold coins in the 1934 gold act. Who owns rare gold coins—people on welfare or rich people? All Americans had to turn in their gold or face a $10,000 fine and up to ten years in prison.

This was an outright confiscation of the gold that was owned by the public. Many were torn between turning it in or hiding it. Those who did turn it in were paid the official price of $20.66 per ounce. This law was so unpopular that no one in the government would admit to creating it. The secretary of the Treasury and FDR said they never read it. It was what the experts wanted. FDR was loved and re-elected many times, but he was a liar and a traitor to us. Maybe this is why presidents are now limited to two four-year terms.

He lied again to the public. "It was necessary to pool the gold to get us out of the Depression. We now know the Depression did not end till after the three-year bear market ended in 1941, then World War II."

FDR built Fort Knox. It was completed in 1936 to store all the stolen gold from the public. In January 1937, the gold began to be deposited there. Once all of the gold was in Fort Knox, the price of gold was raised to $35 per ounce. The huge rip-off was that only foreigners could sell their gold to the Treasury for $35 per ounce. Who has the gold? The international bankers have the gold, which was sold to the Treasury for $35 per ounce. The international bankers almost doubled their money on this transaction. If the Federal Reserve Board is fully controlled by the money changers, who do you think wound up with the gold for free?

Fort Knox would not let anyone near it. Despite many letters from Congress, it was built south of Louisville, Kentucky. On January 13, 1937, military guards and machine guns were posted to protect the gold.

Once all the gold had been illegally confiscated, it was time to start another world war. Moreover, the money changers could create money by controlling the feds and using the fractional reserve method. President Nixon repealed the Gold Reserve Act of 1934 in 1971. The feds started to sell the gold to Russia and other nations for enormous profits. The American people started to buy the gold as well.

World War II put America so deeply in debt that they would never overcome it. It appears to me that the Rothschilds achieved their objective. In 1944 alone, our government spent $183 billion—including $103 billion on the war. The American people incurred 55 percent of the total costs of the war. In addition, other nations involved in the war spent billions.

In 1950, $253 billion was spent. The percentage of debt for those nations involved was a staggering 400 to 1,000 percent. Japan took the biggest hit with over 1,000 percent increase in debt. The Nikkei dropped by 50 percent—from about 40,000—and its commercial real estate was destroyed after falling 60 percent.

After World War I, there were two camps: the communist camp and the capitalistic camp. Both were involved in the profitable arms race. It was time for the money changers to consolidate their position and bring about a world bank. Their plan was to dominate the worldwide economy by

1) centralizing regional economies and European unions
2) centralizing the world economy and world central banks under NAFTA and GATT

NAFTA alone consisted of 14,000 pages. We, in the Reform Party under Ross Perot, fought like cats and dogs all over north, central and south Orange County regions in California to kill the bills. We wrote hundreds of letters to our representatives and senators all to no avail. There were simply too few of us to kill both bills. We knew it was to expedite the new world order.

The International Monetary Fund (IMF) has control of two-thirds of the world's gold. Remember the old rule : he who has the gold makes the rules. The IMF can now manipulate the gold stored at Fort Knox. It was believed that 70 percent of the world's gold was stored in Fort Knox. Congress should have an annual audit for us. However, the Treasury has constantly refused to conduct an audit.

It became very important for us to know the amount of gold that was in—or out of—Fort Knox. We did not want to have the gold standard forced upon us. In other words, have gold back our dollar because we knew it could be easily manipulated. No audit has been conducted since President Eisenhower ordered one in 1953.

The Treasury again refused to allow an audit. Every year, some of the gold was sold to European bankers at $35 per ounce. This was done while it was illegal for Americans to buy gold from Fort Knox. However, corporations and others—such as Firestone—were illegally trading the gold and hid it in Switzerland. They were caught and were successfully prosecuted. Remember, many laws made by our legislators are unconstitutional, and therefore illegal. For instance, if two thirds of the legislators are not assembled (seated), then the law is unconstitutional. This is our Constitution. In addition three fourths of the states must also ratify it. These executive orders must be eliminated they give the president too much power.

By 1971, all the gold had been secretly removed from Fort Knox. In 1971, President Nixon repealed FDR's Gold Reserve Act of 1934. The repeal of that act made it legal for Americans to buy gold. The price of gold immediately started to soar. By 1980, the price of gold was $880 per ounce. This was twenty-five times the price it sold for at Fort Knox. Someone got wind of this and wanted to know who stole the largest fortune in the world. If it was not in Fort Knox, where was it?

Meanwhile, the mysterious death of Louise Auchincloss-Boyer, a key informant and aid to Rockefeller, fell from her tenth-floor apartment in New York City. Accidentally! How convenient for our evil bankers. This silenced the mystery of the stolen gold in Fort Knox. It was later discovered by an article in the newspaper in 1974 that Louise Auchincloss-Boyer was the longtime private secretary of Nelson Rockefeller. Uh oh. It looks like the cat is out of the bag—just as it was with Bill Clinton's secretary, Vince Foster's homicide/suicide. It was also later found that the Rockefellers were manipulating the Federal Reserve Board into selling the gold to anyone, mostly European speculators at bargain basement prices. Mind if I ask a stupid question here? Who got the bucks from the sale of the gold? The gold went from us to Fort Knox to the feds to Europe. I wonder who engineered this deal.

A wealthy industrialist from Ohio took up the quest to solve the Fort Knox mystery. He wrote thousands of letters to the Treasury, bankers, and government about how much gold was stolen and how much was left. He was never successful in his quest.

Edith Roosevelt, the granddaughter of Teddy Roosevelt, also wanted to uncover the truth. She questioned the actions of the government in a March 1975 edition of the New Hampshire Sunday edition. She said, "Allegations of missing gold from our Fort Knox vaults are being widely discussed in European financial circles." It is puzzling that the administration did not demonstrate conclusively that there was no cause for concern over our gold treasure. Naturally, the government would not allow an audit because it would reveal the truth.

In 1980, Ronald Reagan's conservative friends urged him to study the gold standard. He appointed a committee to see if the gold standard would stop government spending. The commission ordered an audit of Fort Knox depository. The audit finally commenced in January 1982. It was determined that there was no gold in Fort Knox. We now know the gold was sold—or given—by the Federal Reserve Board, illegally, to European speculators at bargain prices. Who ordered the feds to sell the gold to European speculators? Not the Rothschilds; they control the feds each time they have their secret meetings.

The feds took our gold, and it was used to pay back our war debts to the international bankers. This was the greatest gold robbery in the world. The public did not realize that our income taxes paid the war debt.

Chapter 35

The IMF, the World Bank, and the BIS

The International Monetary Fund and the World Bank are just across the street from each other in Washington, DC. I don't want to insinuate that all legislators are criminals. A few good representatives truly represent us and realize the extreme importance of doing so. Obviously, these few good representatives can't control Congress, and the bribed leaders have the power and votes over them.

After World War I, people were tired of wars. Under the guise of peacemaking, international bankers later called the money changers created a plan to strengthen their power even more. They pushed forward a plan to create a world government. Their cunning and deceit is unparalleled in history.

The plan was to create a world central bank (the Bank of International Settlement), a judiciary court, and an executive legislature (the League of Nations). This was later called the United Nations.

Carroll Quigley was a professor at Georgetown University (and President Clinton's mentor). In 1956, Quigley wrote a book. The power of financial capitalism had a far reaching plan, nothing less than to create a world system of financial control in private hands able to dominate the political system of each country and the economy of the world as a whole. This system was to be controlled in a feudalistic fashion by the central bankers of the world acting in concert by secret agreements arrived at in frequent meetings and conferences.

The apex of the system was to be the Bank of International Settlement (BIS) in Basel, Switzerland. This private bank would be owned and controlled by the world's central banks, which are private corporations as well.

The central banks sought to dominate the government by controlling Treasury loans, manipulating foreign exchanges, and influencing economic activity in the country. They would also influence cooperative politicians by subsequent rewards in the business world.

Senator Estes Kefauver chaired the House Un-American activities Committee on Un-American Activities in 1954. His committee ferreted out a lot of communists in our country. They have grown in very big bunches since then.

Senator Henry C. Lodge was president of the New York Federal Reserve. He went to Basel with the governor of New York Thomas E. Dewey and bankers to discuss the Versailles Treaty. Senator Lodge would not agree with some points in the treaty. This was the main reason why the US did not join the League of Nations. Without US participation, it would be doomed. The US rejected the BIS until 1945 when the US was officially dragged into it. After that, the world government scheme waned.

International bankers used their old formula and started another world war to wear down the resistance to the World Bank (while creating huge loan profits for themselves). The plan was to resurrect Germany and start another world war. The international bankers would use the capital of the Chase Manhattan Bank, which was controlled by the Rockefeller family. Warburg's Manhattan Bank merged with Chase Bank. Chase Manhattan Bank became the largest bank on Wall Street. This strategy worked, and the world government was finally created. In 1944, the World Bank and the IMF joined together, unfortunately, with full US participation.

Many Americans hated this because they knew how useless it was. They also knew that many nations hated us because of our power, our close ties to Israel, and our interference with their culture and policies.

In World War II, all opposition died—just as the money changers had planned. Here is the hydrogen bomb. The old banking acts gave Congress the power to create fiat world money called special drawing rights (SDRs). The feds created this out of nothing (in excess of $30 billion). Moreover, this world fiat money was fully exchangeable to all world currencies. This was a criminal act by Congress.

In 1968, Congress made laws to accept SDRS. This made them part of our lawful money. Since two-thirds of the world's gold was in the hands of the international bankers, they could manipulate the money for their profits. Just as the feds control the money supply in the US, the IMF, the World Bank, and the BIS controls the world's money supply. These three privately owned corporations are known as the world's central bank.

In 1988, the BIS contracted the reserve of the world banks, through a banking regulation to a whopping 8 percent of liabilities. By 1992, the increased fractional lending put an upper limit on their existing liabilities. This deadly, unlawful banking regulation meant that the banks could not borrow any money till the next economic depression. The banks had to scramble for money to increase their reserves to 8 percent.

In 1988, Japan's banks had the fewest reserves of any country. The Japanese banks were powerless, and their stock market crashed by 50 percent in 1988 and 1989. The Nikkei crashed from above 40,000 to 20,000. In addition, it destroyed commercial real estate, causing it to drop by 60 percent. The Bank of Japan lowered its interest rate to .5 percent. This did not help, and their economy went into a deep depression. This is exactly what is happening to our country now.

The next nation that was affected was Mexico. Its stock exchange—as well as its economy—collapsed. One debt after another was rolled over just to pay the interest on the other. In the south of Mexico, the poor revolted and took their money out of the country to make interest payments. Nations that exchanged their money for SDRs, *the con*, fell into the banker's evil hands.

SDRs are partially backed by gold, which can easily be manipulated by the money changers. The World Central Bank had full control over which nations would receive loans and which would not. This resulted in a steady transfer of wealth from the debtor nations to the World Central Bank. How was this achieved?

In 1992, the third world debtor nations that borrowed from the World Bank paid a horrific 198 million *more* in interest than the developing nations did. By being debtor nations, they subjected themselves to being controlled by the World Bank and its power to inflate or deflate at its discretion and for its own profit. What is happening to Ireland, Spain, France, Italy, and Greece? These nations are in total ruin.

In 1944, the debtor nations reached a staggering $294 billion in debt. This resulted in starvation, poverty, and unemployment.

The entire world faces the same condition by the money changers.

> The third world war has already started. It is a silent war, not for that reason, any less sinister. The war is tearing down Brazil, Latin America, and the third world. Instead of soldiers dying, there are children. It is a war over the third world debt. One, in which has as its main weapon interest, a weapon more deadly than the atom bomb, more shattering than a laser beam.

After World War II, the Bank of England and the Bank of France were both nationalized. However, both were still privately owned, and nothing was accomplished. They continued to grow, be protected by many laws, paid politicians, and be controlled by the media. The media is also in debt to them.

The banks in our country are in a full state of collapse. Many investors in the stock market have liquidated their holdings in banks, causing the banks' stock values to plummet from 50 to 90 percent. Fannie Mae and Freddie Mac, the nation's largest lenders, both went bankrupt—and the stockholders lost out. Both had to be bailed out by the government with taxpayer money. Both are costing us a fortune to keep in business. Many banks are involved in massive foreclosures.

Subprime loans killed the greedy banks. The stock brokerage houses fractionalized them, packaged them into worthless securities, and sold them to investors around the globe. With this, no bank could identify the owners of the foreclosed homes. The banks in possession of the homes had to sell them. In order to do so, the banks had to falsify thousands of documents to illegally complete the sales.

Many homeowners were still in their homes when investors who illegally bought the homes faced the homeowners with illegal documents. The complaints were so massive that Congress had to address the situation. In addition, there were lawsuits galore—from homeowners to buyers—that prevented the buyers from taking possession. This is even after the buyer paid cash for the house. Who was on the banking committee? Chris Dodd and Barney Frank. Both are going into retirement at the same time. These banking heads still get their salaries and bonuses in the many millions of dollars even though they were forced to retire. This also happened to AIG, Merrill Lynch, Bear Stearns, and Lehman Brothers.

Chapter 36

Conclusion and Solutions

We now fully understand the severe problems we have in our country. The only weapon we have is the vote. To continuously vote for the incumbents is the height of stupidity. People should not vote by party only; they should analyze who is running, what their platforms are, and whether they can achieve their goals. The citizens in the Tea Party have taken the first step by voting some of the incumbents out of office and selecting other people to run the government. However, the Tea Party must do much more.

People have to be involved in totally restructuring Congress and how it is organized against us. If the new representatives and senators are not made aware of how Congress is structured, we are doomed. There are career criminals in Congress.

Legislators create the laws and have committees to control them. This gives them inside knowledge about what is going to happen, and they can act upon it for their own profit—and they do. This is one of the many ways they become rich. For instance, if a railroad will be built, they buy the land for peanuts, sell it for a fortune, and pocket the profits. If they know a drug is coming out, they buy stock in the drug company. When the stock increases in value, they sell it for a huge profit.

These situations have made them into multimillionaires. This is illegal. The law against it is the "Insider Trading Fraud Enactment Law of 1988". This is a serious felony with long prison terms and huge fines—except for our legislators. Nobody is above the law, including the legislators. We made them think they are above the law by reelecting them. The public refuses to pay attention to these legislators' laws. Thank god the Tea Party members do.

All the rules have to be completely changed, and most have to be eliminated. Are you aware that thousands of politicians are arrested for taking bribes? We can stop this by voting them out of office. The latest ones are Rep Grimm and Gov. McDonald both were found guilty for taking hundreds of thousands in bribes and sent to prison.

Ten Solutions

1) We can't have leaders in power who will control the House and Senate and be easily bribed. In our country, we have a devastating drug problem and long prison terms. It should be the same way for any politician who takes a bribe. They will not be tried in the Senate because the crooks in the Senate will not convict the crooks because they will rat on each other. There is no honor among thieves. They will be tried for

serious felonies in criminal courts, facing long prison terms and huge fines. Although some have received long prison terms.

2) No legislator can be involved in any business activity—with anyone—directly or indirectly. This includes lobbying. They can only conduct business in Congress, which is what we pay them for. There will be no closed-door meetings. There will be no wars created or deals made behind our backs. Obama raided Medicare to the tune of $716 billion and put it in his health care plan. This was 100% illegal I know I'm in the life insurance business since 1957 to present. The doctors got all shook up and created a copay and coinsurance features in the deal against seniors. The legislator doctors forgot we are paying $105 each month for our health care.

All 285 embassies must be closed immediately. War is very costly, and it is also very profitable for politicians. Who makes and sells war materials to countries? Most important who pockets the money? Where is the money? I didn't get a check did you? Why is Hillary Clinton traveling to all these countries? What secret agreements does she make with them? Hillary probably gets a huge kickback from these agreements. Our politicians don't give money and war materials for free. This is a gimmick to steal our money. Currently it is estimated that about $9.7 trillion of our money is missing. These alleged bailouts are all a hoax. Why? Paying executives multimillion-dollar salaries and bonuses is stupid. They collude with Congress (just as Lincoln stated) to steal our money, and both will split the spoils in one form or another. Fannie Mae and Freddie Mac went bankrupt, costing us billions of dollars, but the executives kept their salaries and bonuses. Something is very wrong here. They must be severely punished since the stockholders lost their entire investment in those issues.

3) We must pull out of the United Nations and not support it because of our relationship with Israel and sticking our nose in many countries business. Who the hell are we to tell another country how to run their policy or culture. Senator John McCain is a liar we are the rulers of the free world. To sanction other nations is a total loss. They will continue to do their thing regardless. Iran and North Korea are prime examples of this. The people of these countries suffer, which will further anger them against us. We can't interfere with other countries' policies or cultures. Senator McCain should not be reelected; he is a maverick progressive who interferes with other countries. He forgot he is a senator for Arizona and not Libya.

4) We must also make sure our troops come home and protect our own borders. The drug crime and murders on our south, bordering Mexico, is

appalling. Our troops will stop the drug cartels dead in their tracks—not to mention that we will be saving a lot of the $1 trillion per year expense as Rep. Ron Paul stated. Some of our politicians hate our soldiers and have stated so. We must immediately increase our military salaries by at least 50 percent, have them pay no income taxes on it, and give them free hospitalization. Our men and women in the service deserve at least this for losing their lives or limbs. What the hell? A lot of minorities, including illegals, get freebies and they don't die or get mutilated in a war. Could this be another vote-grabbing gimmick?

5) We must stop supporting other countries. Let them fend for themselves—just as Syria does. They hate us and tell us right to our face.

   We should only have an import-export relationship with these countries. The trade balance must be a fair one—and not lopsided in favor of the other countries. It is not necessary for them to go overseas—on our nickel—once this embassy business is stopped. They must use their salaries. Now we'll see how lavishly they travel on their nickel. This will stop the lavishness of these career criminals.

6) We would have essentially no employment problem—none if we start drilling for oil and gas on our soil in earnest. They are probably getting huge kickbacks from those foreign oil

nations. No way in heck should it be over $100 per barrel as many nations are selling it for well under $50.00 per barrel. Our oil companies want the oil to stay high so they can continue their huge profits and taxes for our thug government. In any event, we are now the largest exporters of oil products. This may mean the death of the OPEC as far as us importing a large amount of oil from them. We would do well to boycott one oil company for a month. This will bring them to their knees. In any event the world depression has caused the oil to drop by 64%. This is very bullish for our country as it reduces costs down the line and therefore non-inflationary.

We have an incredible amount of oil and gas. By immediately starting drilling it in earnest on land and continuing with the XL Pipeline, we will put at least 10 millions of Americans to work with high wages. That lying dog N.Y. senator Schumer was dead wrong about his low ball figure of 3500 being employed on the XL pipeline. That's all he does is lie about that and his opponents. This can be achieved by eliminating the tax on our businesses so they can train the people to work for them. The housing and automobile industries will take off and soar out of sight, employing even more people. This is not happening now because the career criminals are protecting their political parties and positions.

We have now totally reversed our situation. Our fuel needs will not be dependent on any foreign imports. The manipulation by our own oil companies and Congress will come to an end. There is to be no red tape on this project whatsoever. We must zero in on those who oppose it as it means our very livelihood. They must have some ulterior evil motive in opposing it. In addition, we must build more nuclear power plants because they are so efficient to operate. France has proven this over decades. One major problem is how to dispose of the nuclear waste or use it for another purpose.

7) Salaries for our legislators must be immediately reduced to $100,000 for those over—or increased to $100,000 for those under—per year with no perks whatsoever. They can only raise their salary by using the CPI index. This is the consumer price index that they use for us. congress cheats us by not including food and energy, which are the two most inflationary items. Congress can't play games with this twelve-indicator index because it will apply to them as well. Now that oil has dropped sharply you will see prices also drop as the cost of shipping will drop. This will also contain inflation as well.

How do the legislators obtain their compensation? Watch them vote for their compensation at midnight on C-SPAN 1 or 2. We are the dummies who let them do this by re-electing them. We pay them. They are our servants. Since when do you tell your boss you raised your salary last night? See how stupid we are by not figuring this out? Congress did not give seniors a CPI increase in 2010. The increase for 2011 was 1.7%, 2012 was 3.6 percent, 2013 1.7% same for 2014. Of course *all americans new this.* Ha, ha, ha.

8) Bureaucracy is is an extremely important area. Most bureaucrats are substantially overpaid for what they do. A huge amount of tax dollars are totally wasted in these bureaus. The government accounting office (GAO) recently issued a 345-page report on the duplication of at least forty-five departments, wasting billions of dollars of taxpayer money. I have noticed and stated this for years. Our government has overstepped our Constitution; in doing so, it has unlawfully interfered with every facet of our lives. Our government should have absolutely nothing to do with banking, insurance, stock market, businesses, or anything else outside of government. Our economy is so vast and complex that it must operate in the free marketplace.

   These bureaus overregulate businesses and people, and they squeeze businesses and people to death financially with excessive taxes and regulations. I am a supply-sider proponent as was Ron Reagan and Jack Kemp. The monetary theory is deadly and does not work at all. Supply and demand works very well. When the demand for oil goes down, the stockpile goes up—and the price goes down. It is now manipulated to an extreme and should be at best only $50 per barrel. This will happen to anything else that gets too pricey.

The free marketplace will automatically take care of it; nothing has to be done or manipulated. Our government has millions of employees, most in these duplicating agencies. We must close them over a period of time and employ the laid-off workers in some form of private industry.

Disbanding the IRS eliminates the tax burden on businesses and gives them more than enough money to start hiring and training employees. No red tape. This must be done now.

9) A national retail sales tax system will replace the IRS. When the GAO audited the IRS, the IRS could not account for two-thirds of the money it collected in taxes. This is why your income tax check is paid to the US Treasury and not the IRS. Only nine states have to be added to the sales tax system. We must in no uncertain terms demand that our new legislators eliminate IRS. In order for this to work, we must not reelect any incumbent who opposes this. This will take time because the newly elected officials must be in the majority—and therefore have the

majority voting power to accomplish it. There will be no more committees representing any of our industries because there will be no need to control the various businesses any longer. Creating committees to investigate serious complaints is okay. However, this should be minimal. The NRSTS is our true solution in controlling our money.

Here is how it will function. The sales tax will be 15 percent and 20 percent for luxury items. Food will not be taxed. Since it is a state tax only, the states can increase the tax with a state referendum by the people outlining a specific project(s) and put in a trust fund. What you earn, you keep—100 percent. This includes earned and unearned income. In other words, we keep it all. When we buy anything, we know exactly what the tax is. The sales tax on a house will be spread over the life of the mortgage.

Most Americans will not invest their money to have unearned income. Investing takes time, money, and concentration. Therefore, very few will undertake investing.

The national retail sales tax system is awesome for the states because the sales tax will soar out of sight because of spendaholic citizens. Why? Most states are broke. The same rules apply to officials of cities, counties, and states. Each of them will be able to function without federal intervention. In addition, they must subcontract a lot of work to outside firms. Why pay employees horrific salaries, pensions, and benefits when outside firms are capable of doing most of the work? These officials and managers of cities, counties and states must be frugal, create surpluses, and maintain surpluses to prevent future *shortfalls*. If they do not do so, they must be replaced on re-election.

10) Reduce and eliminate debt. We have six denominations of dollars—one, five, ten, twenty, fifty, and one hundred. Has anyone besides me bothered to read them in detail? Nope. On the top it says, "Federal Reserve note." On the left side, above the black circle, it says, "This note is legal tender for all debts, public and private." Our government can start to reduce our borrowing by selling fewer T-bills, T-notes, and T-bonds. Each week, T-bills and T-notes are sold or bought by the feds. Each month, T-bonds are bought or sold by the feds. All three bills are in multibillion dollar amounts.

Even though the government prints billions of dollars, they can't use this money to reduce our debt. They must use it to pay their bills and debt interest. What bills? Eliminating many bureaus that the states should have will reduce their bills and free those dollars to pay down the debt just as President Jackson did. Our obese government must be reduced to its minimal size.

The automatic debt reduction came into play automatically when Congress could not agree on a debt reduction. The evil ones are the very sick Harry Reid who can hardly talk or walk and the mentally retarded Pelosi and others. This is why our government refuses to do a budget. It would reveal the bribes and all other criminal activities they are involved in. Eliminating all of it would put us on a sound fiscal basis.

Finally, we can't do this on a one-by-one basis. We must be as organized as the lying and deceitful career criminals. The Tea Party is organized. Join them so we can coordinate our activities and take over and control Congress and the administration rather than having them control us, which is now the case. Put your two cents in so you can be heard. Each of us is important—and so is our vote. Use it wisely. Above all, do not vote by party. Who are you voting for? What is his or her background? Is he or she qualified? Our country is not a candy store. It is vast and complex and requires qualified, honest people to run it. We therefore must be very careful when selecting our politicians.

Is President Obama qualified to run our country? Only three years in the Senate and a community organizer for about twenty years. Not gainfully employed during that time. He obviously had no foreign policy experience. What possible reason could most of the minorities including our juniors and seniors who voted for him have?